Gennaro's
ITALIAN
BAKERY

Gennaro's ITALIAN BAKERY

GENNARO CONTALDO

PHOTOGRAPHY BY DAN JONES

PAVILION

TO ADRIANA AND LIZ

CONTENTS

INTRODUCTION

When I first heard that my publisher was interested in doing a book about bread and baking, I was so excited! Baking, especially bread, has always been my passion – in fact if my career hadn't gone down the route it has, I would have been a baker. Those three simple ingredients – flour, yeast, water – and what they are transformed into has always fascinated me. Even as a young boy, I would spend hours at my uncle's bakery just watching as he mixed, kneaded, pulled, shaped and baked, pushing and turning loaves in and out of his big wood-fired oven. The smell was irresistible and I couldn't wait to taste whatever *panino* he would let me have. My mother also baked, usually once a week, and on that morning I would awake to that dreamy smell of home baking that made me jump out of bed ravenous and run into the warmth of the smoke-filled kitchen.

When I worked at The Neal Street Restaurant and later at my own restaurant, I would arrive very early – in fact often during the night – so I could do the day's baking – bread, focaccia, *torte salate*, perhaps pastry for *crostata* depending on the day's menu, and seasonal bakes like *Pastiera di Grano* at Easter or *Panettoncini* at Christmas. I loved starting my day like this – it was like a ritual – from lighting the ovens, mixing the yeast, watching those bubbles appear, leaving the dough to rise and that magical moment when the baked goodies came out of the oven.

For me baking is an almost magical process; it never ceases to amaze me that a few simple basic ingredients mixed together and placed in the oven produce such incredible, mouth-watering delicacies the world over craves. Take cakes, for instance, that mushy mixture made up in a bowl transforms itself into something wonderful, giving pleasure to many – it may be for a birthday or just simply to enjoy at teatime, but is always a joy.

There is always a kind of excitement when baking for whatever reason or occasion, an anticipation of how the bread, cake, biscuits, focaccia or pie will turn out and the smells of home baking are heavenly, filling the house with a warm feeling and irresistible aroma no air freshener can ever match! Whether you bake or not, are an expert or just like to try a recipe from time to time, I think everyone loves the idea of home baking. Young children love to experiment with dough or pastry and make their own shapes, or help mix a cake and then lick the spoon! The taste of any home-baked product can never be matched by commercially produced goods.

Wherever I am in Italy, I always like to check out the local *panetteria* (bakery), or in smaller villages known as *forno* (oven), to see which delicious regional varieties they offer, and not only bread but focaccia, *torte salate*, tarts, biscuits and cakes. I never leave empty-handed and love to try their specialities. Local bakeries in Italy bake all their own goods in the back and are often family-run from generations so you know what you are consuming is good-quality home-produced stuff. Some larger *panetterie*, especially in bigger towns and cities, offer drinks and you can sit or stand at the counter to enjoy an espresso and brioche at breakfast or a pizzetta for a quick lunch.

Traditionally, the *forno* or *panetteria* (bakery) was a place for locals to meet up, especially in small towns and villages. Not everyone had an oven at home, so it was quite normal for housewives to make the bread dough and perhaps other baked goods and take them along to the bakery to be baked in the wood-fired oven. Lots of people did this, so a different mark would be made on each loaf so it could be returned to the right person. I remember this was still quite common when I was a little boy and the bakery was always a busy place. The families who owned pieces of land for the purpose of growing their own produce often had an oven built nearby so they could do their baking there as well as work on their allotment.

Although all the recipes in this book have been tested in an electric fan-assisted oven, I love the old wood-fired ovens, so a few years ago, I had one built in my garden. I love baking bread and pizza in it – the smell and taste transport me back to my childhood days.

Bread and baked goods mean tradition. And bakeries honour these traditions when certain breads and baked goods are made to celebrate the feast day of a local patron saint or during festivities like Christmas, Easter and *Carnevale*. Each region has its own roots which once symbolised a ritual or perhaps were made for nobility or even came about as *cucina povera* (poor man's food) – now those specialities are symbols of that tradition and have become part of that town's or region's culture. And quite often a town will be famous for that particular product and *Sagre* (food festivals) are held in honour of it.

I love the history of how a foodstuff has evolved and in Italy there are so many stories, but to include them all would mean writing volumes. So in this book I would like to share a selection of my favourite easy to create recipes for products which can be found in a typical Italian bakery – some traditional, some unusual to a particular area and some with a modern twist.

Enjoy and Happy Baking!

FLOURS

FOR MAKING BREAD, PIZZA, FOCACCIA AND PAN DOLCI

Use a good-quality strong bread flour which has more protein and is ideal for bread making. I like to use strong Canadian flour, available from good supermarkets.

I also use Italian Manitoba 00 flour, which has a high protein content and is available from good Italian delis and online. This should not to be confused with '00' flour for pasta making. Always check what is written on the packet and make sure it is suitable for bread making before using.

Semola di grano duro rimacinata (hard durum wheat semolina) is good for rustic breads, such as Altamura, giving the bread its classic yellow colour. Again, this flour can be found in good Italian delis or online.

FOR PASTRIES AND BISCUITS

A good-quality plain flour which is made with softer wheats, widely available. I have noticed a lot of brands now specify on their packets what the flour is suitable for, so always check on the label before buying.

FOR CAKES

A good-quality self-raising flour. Alternatively, you can add baking powder to plain flour. In Italy baking powder is sold in sachets known as *lievito per dolci* (raising agent for cakes). Again, always check the packets before using.

GLUTEN-FREE FLOUR

Doves do an excellent range of gluten-free flours for bread and other baking purposes as well as a gluten-free baking powder.

Chickpea, chestnut, rice, potato, polenta and almond flours are all gluten-free, however, don't just substitute these with regular flours as whatever you are making may not turn out as well as you wanted it to be. A lot of these flours have to be mixed with other flours to obtain the correct strength and consistency, so always follow the recipes when making gluten-free and check the labels on packets. Recipes that are totally gluten-free are highlighted in this book.

YEAST

Yeast is an organism of the fungus family which is used as a rising agent in breads and other baked goods that require the dough to rise. For the dough to rise, the yeast needs to grow, and for this it requires a combination of moisture, warmth and food. Yeast is alive and needs to be treated correctly – that is why lukewarm water or milk is used to dissolve the yeast before it is added to the flour. Yeast comes in three forms – fresh, dried and fast-action easy blend.

FRESH YEAST

I like to use fresh yeast and find that it produces the best results. It can be bought from bakeries and supermarkets with an in-store bakery. I find it such a shame that fresh yeast is not more easily available in this country. In Italy, most supermarkets sell 25g/1oz packaged cubes of fresh yeast in their fridge section, which is perfect for domestic use. Here it is usually sold in large blocks so what you don't use, you should wrap very tightly in clingfilm and store in the refrigerator for up to two weeks. If you freeze fresh yeast, make sure it is tightly wrapped and it will probably keep for up to a month.

DRIED YEAST AND FAST-ACTION EASY BLEND

Despite my preference for fresh, I always keep some dried yeast in my storecupboard. These are fresh yeasts which have been dried and are much more concentrated than the fresh variety. Dried yeast is usually sold in small tins and needs to be dissolved in the same way as fresh yeast.

The fast-action yeast is usually sold in 7g/¼oz sachets and combined with flour before adding the liquid.

I have used fresh yeast throughout this book, but if you don't have it, then please do use the dried variety, but always check the instructions on the label for quantities before using.

BIGA

A *biga* (starter dough) has been used in Italian bread making since yeast has been around. It helps boost the performance of bread as well as adding a light open texture and maintaining the bread for longer. It is made daily with a tiny amount of fresh yeast, water and the same flour which the bread will be made out of. Extra fresh yeast is also added to speed up rising times; however, bread can be made with just the *biga* as long as it is left to rise for longer. This is my version of an Italian *biga* used to make Puglian Bread (see p.48).

2g/under ⅛oz fresh yeast
150ml/5fl oz/⅔ cup lukewarm water
120g/4½oz/1 cup strong white bread flour or semolina

Dissolve the yeast in the lukewarm water. Put the flour on a clean work surface, add the yeast mixture and mix until it is well incorporated. Cover with clingfilm and leave at room temperature for 24 hours before using.

COOKING NOTES

• Making egg wash – Lightly beat 1 egg yolk and 1 tablespoon of milk together in a bowl.

 • Preparing tins – All the tins can be greased with either a little oil or softened or melted butter. If the tins need lining, then use either parchment or baking paper.

• Resting dough – When resting dough, ideally it should be left in the oven with the light on.

PANE Bread

For me, there is no other foodstuff more satisfying and complete than bread. It has been a staple in most countries of the world for thousands of years. There was a time when people had bread to eat and little else; it is one of the most basic foods of human life.

Italians take bread very seriously – it is present at every meal – from dunking into milky coffee at breakfast to accompanying all courses during lunch and dinner. And the traditional *merenda* (teatime snack) for children after school has always been *pane, burro e marmelata* (bread, butter and jam). If, for any reason, fresh bread is not available, Italians always keep a storecupboard supply of *grissini, taralli, freselle* or other hard-baked bread substitutes, just in case.

Bread also forms a vital part of the Italian food culture and is intertwined in many local traditions, rituals, feasts and religious festivities. Traditionally, festive breads were made on the day the village celebrated its patron saint; volunteers would go from door to door with big baskets filled with votive breads in exchange for an offering. Bread and religion are closely linked and bread is said to be a gift from God. This is probably why leftover bread is never wasted and it is considered bad luck to throw it away, so any leftovers are made into breadcrumbs or used up in other culinary ways. There are even whole museums dedicated to this humble but important foodstuff throughout Italy – in Trapani Sicily, Cosenza and in Sardinia.

It is said Italy produces over 1500 types of bread. Every region, town, village and even bakery has its own specialities, whether it's the way the bread is cooked, left to rise, the type of flour or the shape of the loaf, the varieties are endless and fascinating. Probably the most famous is the *Pane di Altamura* – bread from the little town in Puglia which a few years ago made international news when locals fought to close down McDonalds in favour of a bakery. The rustic loaf is made with local hard durum wheat *semola* flour, is a lovely yellow colour with a hard crust, and has been made a Denomación de Origen (DOP) protected product. There is also the *Pane di Genzano*, a town outside Rome, whose soft white loaf covered with wheat bran has also been given DOP status.

There is nothing more pleasurable than making your own bread and the aroma from the oven from a freshly baked loaf is one of the best. It is so simple to make a standard traditional loaf – flour, yeast, salt and water – which forms the basis of most breads including the popular *grissini* (breadsticks), which are so often found on the Italian table at mealtimes for anyone preferring a light and crunchy alternative.

For the next step up, enriched breads, like *Casatiello*, which is made in southern Italy at Easter, are made perhaps for a special occasion and packed with lots of other ingredients. Italians are also now experimenting with age-old grains like spelt, buckwheat, and adding seeds to their dough for a healthier approach.

Traditionally, bread is made with a *biga* (starter), which is still used in Italian bakeries. A small amount of dough from the previous day's baking is kept and added to start a new dough. The *biga*, or *la Madre* (mother) as it is sometimes referred to, starts with flour and water and is left to ferment naturally for a long time, or sometimes organic plain yogurt can be added or a tiny amount of yeast to speed up the process.

THE STAGES OF BREAD MAKING

MIXING

This is when you combine the basic ingredients – usually flour and salt – then pour in the yeast mixture and remaining liquid. Mix with either a wooden spoon or, as I prefer, by hand, until all the ingredients are well incorporated and form into a dough. All the recipes in this book have been tried and tested; however, you may find you need to add a little more or less liquid – sometimes weather humidity plays an important factor. If you find you have added all the liquid and it is too much, simply add a little flour.

KNEADING

This is the process of manipulating the dough so the yeast is evenly distributed and the proteins in the flour develop the gluten. Lightly flour a work surface and place the dough on it. Place the heel of your hand on top of the dough and push away from you. Using your fingertips, flip the dough over, pulling the dough back towards you. Continue doing this, alternating hands, for about 10 minutes or as specified in the recipe. To see if a dough has been kneaded for long enough, roll it tightly into a ball, poke it with your finger – if it springs back readily and has a smooth appearance, it is ready. Some enriched doughs, such as brioche, can be very sticky, so these are easier made in a mixing bowl or in a freestanding mixer with the dough hook attachment.

RISING

This is the stage when the dough is set to rest so that it can expand. Place the ball of dough into a large bowl, cover with either a cloth or clingfilm, and leave in a warm place. This can be near a source of heat, the linen cupboard, warm utility room or in the oven with just the light on. On a hot day, it can be left anywhere in the kitchen. Follow rising times as stated in the recipes; however, you may find that you need a little shorter or longer. Basically an hour should suffice for normal bread dough, but the general rule is until the dough has doubled in size. Be careful the dough could also over-rise and collapse. If this happens, knead the dough for a few minutes and leave to rise again. You can make dough in advance, cover it with clingfilm and store it in the refrigerator, where it will rise very slowly, and then use it when required.

KNOCKING BACK AND SHAPING

This is when you take the dough and 'knock back' all the air bubbles that have been created during rising. If you didn't do this, the dough would eventually collapse. To knock back, you simply knead again but only for a couple of minutes. Sometimes the recipe requires other ingredients and this is the time to knead them in until they are well incorporated.

It is now time to shape the dough, whether it is a whole loaf or individual rolls. To divide the dough into pieces, use a dough cutter. Once the dough has been shaped, place in the prepared baking tin.

PROVING

This is the final rising before the dough is baked. Loosely cover the dough and leave to rest in a warm place. Proving time should not take as long as the first rising; however, check the recipe and do not allow to overproof. The dough should be well risen, feel soft and spongy, and if you prod with your finger the dough will spring back slowly. During this time, preheat the oven.

BAKING

This is when the bread goes into the oven – make sure the oven is hot and at the correct temperature. At the beginning of baking, the dough continues to rise due to the formation of steam and stops when the dough hardens and the yeast dies. Check the baking times of your recipe but all ovens are different and timings can vary slightly. For the purpose of this book, all the recipes have been tested in a fan oven. Basically a loaf of bread is ready when it is golden brown all over and sounds hollow when tapped underneath. If the top has browned too quickly, place some foil over or, if possible, turn over the bread on its side and continue to bake. Remove from the oven and leave to cool on a wire rack before eating.

This is my version of a basic bread loaf. With just basic ingredients and so simple to make, there is no reason why it can't be made every day.

BASIC BREAD DOUGH

Serves 6

semolina, for sprinkling
12g/just under ½oz fresh yeast
350ml/12fl oz/1½ cups lukewarm water
500g/1lb 2oz/4 cups strong white bread flour
8g/just under ¼oz/1¼ tsp salt

Sprinkle a flat baking tray with semolina.

Dissolve the yeast in the lukewarm water. Combine the flour and salt on a clean work surface, then gradually add the yeast liquid, mixing with your hands until a soft dough forms. Knead the dough for 10 minutes until smooth and elastic. Place the dough in a large bowl, cover with a cloth and leave to rest in a warm place for 1 hour, or until it has doubled in size.

Knock the dough back down and shape into a round loaf or whichever shape you prefer (see overleaf for shaping ideas – there are many traditional shapes you can try). Place on the prepared baking tray, cover with a cloth and leave to rise again for 30 minutes.

Meanwhile, preheat the oven to 220°C (fan)/240°C/475°F/Gas mark 9.

Bake the bread on the bottom shelf of the oven for 30 minutes. The best way to test if the loaf is ready is to bang it gently on the base; if it sounds hollow, the bread is ready. Remove from the oven and leave to cool.

This bread is delicious eaten on the day it is made. However, if stored correctly, it will keep for a few days and is delicious toasted, used to make bruschetta or made into breadcrumbs.

Grissini were first made in Turin in the 1600s for the son of a duke who was unable to eat bread. Since then, they have become a firm favourite in the Italian bread basket, especially popular with dieting ladies preferring the lighter, crispier breadstick to a bread roll. In Italy, artisan-produced *grissini* bought from good bakery shops can be as long as 80cm/31½in; some have a twisty pattern and some are long and skinny. I like to make my own *grissini* as they can be kept for longer and make a lovely snack at any time. They are delicious wrapped with slices of prosciutto and served with drinks or as part of an antipasto. This is my version of plain *grissini* – you can also add flavours, see p.26 and p.27

GRISSINI – PLAIN
Breadsticks

Makes about 24

15g/½oz fresh yeast
280ml/9½fl oz/1¼ cups lukewarm water
250g/9oz/2 cups strong white bread flour
250g/9oz/scant 1½ cups durum wheat semolina
    flour, plus extra for sprinkling
10g/¼oz/1½ tsp salt
4 tbsp extra virgin olive oil

Dissolve the yeast in the lukewarm water. Combine the flour, semolina and salt. Pour in the extra virgin olive oil and gradually add the yeast mixture, mixing well to make a dough. Knead the dough for 5 minutes, then cover with a cloth and leave to rest in a warm place for 20 minutes.

Roll out the dough on a lightly floured work surface to a rough square. Lightly brush with a little water and sprinkle a handful of semolina. Using a pastry cutter or sharp knife, cut out strips about 2cm/¾in wide. Don't worry about the length, as they can be different sizes.

Sprinkle some semolina on a baking tray, then place the *grissini* on the tray, gently pulling at either side as you place them down. Space them about 2cm/¾in apart. If you want the *grissini* to have a roundish shape, roll each strip gently with your fingers before placing them on the baking tray. Leave to rest in a warm place for 30 minutes.

Preheat the oven to 220°C (fan)/240°C/475°F/Gas mark 9.

Bake the *grissini* in the oven for 10 minutes. Remove from the oven and turn the oven down to 100°C (fan)/110°C/212°F/Gas mark ¼. Once this temperature is reached, put the *grissini* back in for 40 minutes or until golden brown. Remove from the oven and leave to cool.

The addition of Parmesan makes these very moreish indeed.

GRISSINI AL PARMIGGIANO
Parmesan Breadsticks

Makes about 24

15g/½oz fresh yeast
280ml/9½fl oz/1¼ cups lukewarm water
250g/9oz/2 cups strong white bread flour
250g/9oz/scant 1½ cups durum wheat semolina
   flour, plus extra for sprinkling
10g/¼oz/1½ tsp salt
85g/3oz/¾ cup grated Parmesan cheese
4 tbsp extra virgin olive oil ,

Dissolve the yeast in the lukewarm water. Combine the flour, semolina, salt and grated Parmesan. Pour in the extra virgin olive oil and gradually add the yeast mixture mixing well to make a dough. Knead for 5 minutes, then cover with a cloth and leave to rest for 20 minutes.

Roll out the dough on a lightly floured work surface to a rough square. Lightly brush with a little water and sprinkle a handful of semolina. Using a pastry cutter or sharp knife, cut out strips about 2cm/¾in wide. Don't worry about the length, as they can be different sizes.

Sprinkle some semolina on a baking tray. Place the *grissini* on the tray gently pulling at either side as you place them down. Space them about 2cm/¾in apart. If you want the *grissini* to have a roundish shape, roll each strip gently with your fingers before placing them on the baking tray. Leave to rest in a warm place for 30 minutes.

Preheat the oven at 220°C (fan)/240°C/475°F/Gas mark 9.

Bake the *grissini* in the oven for 10 minutes. Remove from the oven and turn the oven down to 100°C (fan)/110°C/212°F/Gas mark ¼. Wait for the oven to reach this temperature, then put the *grissini* back in for 40 minutes or until golden brown. Remove from the oven and leave to cool.

Some chopped mixed herbs are added for an extra kick and colour.

GRISSINI ALLE ERBE
Mixed Herb Breadsticks

Makes about 24

15g/½oz fresh yeast
180ml/6fl oz/¾ cup lukewarm water
250g/9oz/2 cups strong white bread flour
250g/9oz/scant 1½ cups durum wheat semolina
   flour, plus extra for sprinkling
10g/¼oz/1½ tsp salt
needles of 1 rosemary branch, finely chopped
handful of thyme leaves, finely chopped
8 sage leaves, finely chopped
4 tbsp extra virgin olive oil

Dissolve the yeast in the lukewarm water. Combine the flour, semolina, salt and herbs. Pour in the extra virgin olive oil and gradually add the yeast mixture, mixing well to make a dough. Knead for 5 minutes, then cover with a cloth and leave to rest for 20 minutes.

Roll out the dough on a lightly floured work surface to a rough square. Lightly brush with a little water and sprinkle a handful of semolina. Using a pastry cutter or sharp knife, cut out strips about 2cm/¾in wide. Don't worry about the length, as they can be different sizes.

Sprinkle some semolina on a baking tray. Place the *grissini* on the tray, gently pulling at either side as you place them down. Space them about 2cm/¾in apart. If you want the *grissini* to have a roundish shape, roll each strip gently with your fingers before placing them on the baking tray. Leave to rest in a warm place for 30 minutes.

Preheat the oven at 220°C (fan)/240°C/475°F/Gas mark 9.

Bake the *grissini* in the oven for 10 minutes. Remove from the oven and turn the oven down to 100°C (fan)/110°C/212°F/Gas mark ¼. Wait for the oven to reach this temperature, then put the *grissini* back in for 40 minutes or until golden brown. Remove from the oven and leave to cool.

I love experimenting with bread, and the addition of ricotta to the dough gives this bread its light texture. The chopped sage leaves give it a mildly pleasant aroma, but could be omitted if you prefer or more added for a stronger flavour. It is delicious sliced and spread with butter or eaten with some bread and cheese for a delicious snack.

TRECCIA CON RICOTTA E SALVIA
Plaited Loaf with Ricotta and Sage

Serves 6–8

12g/just under ½oz fresh yeast
200ml/7fl oz/scant 1 cup lukewarm water
250g/9oz/scant 1½ cups durum wheat semolina flour, plus extra for sprinkling
250g/9oz/2 cups strong white bread flour
160g/5¾oz/¾ cup ricotta
2 tsp runny honey
6g/¼oz/1 tsp salt
10 small sage leaves, finely chopped

Line a large flat baking tray with parchment paper.

Dissolve the yeast in the lukewarm water. Combine the flours on a clean work surface, then make a well in the centre and add the ricotta, yeast mixture, honey, salt and sage. Mix together to make a dough, then knead for 10 minutes. Form the dough into a ball, cover with clingfilm and leave to rest in a warm place for 1 hour 30 minutes, or until doubled in size.

Divide the dough into 3 equal pieces. Roll out each piece into a long sausage shape about 50cm/20in long and form these into a plait. Place on the prepared baking tray, cover with a cloth and leave to rest for a further 1 hour 30 minutes.

Preheat the oven to 200°C (fan)/220°C/425°F/Gas mark 7.

Sprinkle a little flour all over the loaf and bake in the oven for 35 minutes.

Remove from the oven, leave to cool, then slice and enjoy.

These lovely, super-soft milk rolls are ideal for children or the elderly who may find it difficult to chew crusty bread. In Italy, for a treat, the rolls are often filled with Nutella or jam as an after-school snack or at children's parties. The addition of seeds as a topping makes them nice and healthy too. If you prefer, you can omit the seeds, but I love them.

PANINI AL LATTE
Milk Rolls

Makes 12

12g fresh yeast
½ tsp caster (superfine) sugar
160ml/5½fl oz/scant ¾ cup lukewarm milk
350g/12oz/scant 3 cups strong white bread flour
½ tsp salt
1 egg, beaten
50g/1¾oz/3½ tbsp butter, softened at
    room temperature
1 egg yolk and a little milk mixed together
    for brushing
a few sesame seeds, pumpkin seeds, sunflower
    seeds or seeds of your choice

Line a flat baking tray with parchment paper.

Dissolve the yeast and sugar in the lukewarm milk. Combine the flour and salt, then mix in the egg and butter. Gradually add the yeast mixture, mixing well with your hands, then knead for 10 minutes to make a soft dough. Form into a ball, cover with a cloth and leave to rest in a warm place for 1½ hours, or until it has doubled in size.

Knead the dough for 2 minutes, then divide it into 12 pieces. Roll each piece with your hands into a sausage, then roll the sausage into a snail shape. Place each roll on the prepared baking tray, cover with a cloth and leave to rest in a warm place for 30 minutes.

Preheat the oven to 200°C (fan)/220°C/425°F/Gas mark 7.

Mix the egg yolk and milk together, brush over the rolls and top with seeds of your choice. Bake in the oven for 15–20 minutes until golden.

Remove from the oven, leave to cool and enjoy!

This bread dates back to ancient Naples when the official language for the rich was French but for the general population it was *cafone*, meaning peasant. The name was given to this popular bread eaten by the poorer Neapolitans of that time. Very simple to prepare with no kneading required, the dough is left to rest for 24 hours. It was traditionally cooked in a wood-oven, but works just as well inside a cast-iron pot (Le Creuset type) – make sure it is deep enough as the bread has to have plenty of room to cook inside with the lid on. I love the crackling sound it makes when you take it out of the oven! The texture of the bread is lovely and light inside with a wonderful crust on the outside – it reminds me of how bread used to taste when I was a young boy in Italy.

PANE CAFONE
Neapolitan Peasant Bread

Serves 4

3g/just under ⅛oz fresh yeast
250ml/9fl oz/generous 1 cup lukewarm water
375g/13oz/3 cups strong white bread flour
7g/¼oz/generous 1 tsp salt

Dissolve the yeast in the lukewarm water. Place 300g/10½oz/scant 2½ cups of the flour on a clean work surface, add the yeast mixture and mix in gently with a spoon. Combine the remaining flour with the salt in a bowl, then add this to the flour and yeast mixture, gently mixing until all the ingredients are well amalgamated (you may need a little more water, so add it very carefully). Cover with clingfilm and leave to rest in a warm place for 24 hours. After a few hours, small bubbles will appear on the dough and this is perfectly normal.

After 24 hours, place the dough on a lightly floured work surface and gently fold over a couple of times into a ball. Cover with a clean cloth and leave to rest for 2 hours.

After 1 hour, preheat the oven to 220°C (fan)/240°C/475°F/Gas mark 9 and place an empty cast-iron pot (without lid) in the oven.

Remove the pot from the oven and carefully place the bread inside. Make a couple of incisions on the top of the dough, cover with the lid and place immediately inside the oven on the bottom shelf. Bake for 30 minutes. Remove the lid and continue to bake for 15 minutes.

Remove from the oven, leave in the pot for 10 minutes, then turn out of the pot onto a wire rack and leave to cool completely. Slice and enjoy!

This rich savoury bread, also known as *tortano*, is traditionally made at Easter time in the Naples area. The ingredients and method have religious connotations; the rising of the dough means new life, the shape symbolises Christ's crown of thorns and eggs are rebirth. There are many variations of this bread and each town, village and family have their own favourites – what they all have in common is the richness of the substantial ingredients that go into this bread, making it a meal in itself. I remember, when I lived in Italy, we would often take this bread with us on the traditional Easter Monday picnic and a slice or two was really all you needed. For the cured meats, try to get them in chunks so you can cut them into cubes.

CASATIELLO
Neapolitan Easter Bread

Serves 10

30g/1oz fresh yeast
300ml/10fl oz/1¼ cups lukewarm water
500g/1lb 2oz/4 cups strong white bread flour
1 tsp salt
1 tsp black pepper
50g/1¾oz/scant ½ cup grated Parmesan cheese
50g/1¾oz/scant ½ cup grated pecorino cheese
100ml/3½fl oz/scant ½ cup extra virgin olive oil
50g/1¾oz prosciutto piece, cut into small cubes
50g/1¾oz mortadella piece, cut into small cubes
50g/1¾oz salami piece, cut into small cubes
50g/1¾oz provolone (or mature Cheddar) cheese,
     cut into small cubes
5 hard-boiled eggs, 2 cut into quarters
     and 3 left whole

Lightly grease a 26cm/10½in ring tin.

Dissolve the yeast in the lukewarm water. Combine the flour, salt, pepper, Parmesan and pecorino on a clean work surface. Add the extra virgin olive oil, then gradually add the yeast mixture, mixing well with your hands to form a dough. Knead for 5 minutes, then cover with a cloth and leave to rest in a warm place for 1 hour, or until doubled in size.

Spread the dough out on a lightly floured work surface into a roughly rectangular shape. Arrange the cured meats, cheese and egg quarters all over. Place the 3 whole eggs on one of the longer sides and carefully roll into a large sausage, pressing gently so the filling doesn't escape.

Carefully place into the prepared ring tin, sealing the 2 sides well together. Cover with a cloth and leave to rest in a warm place for 2 hours, or until doubled in size.

Meanwhile, preheat the oven to 180°C (fan)/200°C/400°F/Gas mark 6.

Bake the *Casatiello* for 1 hour. Remove from the oven, leave to cool, then turn out of the tin and enjoy warm or cold.

It is quite common to go to a bakery in Italy and specifically ask for *panini all'olio* (olive oil rolls). Soft and light, these rolls are a pleasure to eat either plain or filled with some cured meats or cheese for a lovely lunch or snack. Kept in an airtight container, they will keep for a couple of days.

PANINI ALL'OLIO
Olive Oil Rolls

Makes about 16

18g/¾oz fresh yeast
250ml/9fl oz/generous 1 cup lukewarm water
50ml/2fl oz/scant ¼ cup olive oil
1 egg yolk
6g/¼oz/1 tsp caster (superfine) sugar
500g/1lb 2oz/4 cups strong white bread flour, sifted
15g/½oz/2½ tsp salt

Line a large flat baking tray with parchment paper.

Combine the yeast with the lukewarm water and olive oil. Stir in the egg yolk, sugar and half of the flour. Add the salt, then the remaining flour and mix well to make a dough. Turn out onto a work surface and knead for about 5 minutes. Place the dough in a large bowl, cover with clingfilm and leave to rest in a warm place for 1 hour, or until doubled in size.

Divide the dough into pieces, about 50g/1¾oz, then shape into round or long rolls or whatever shape you prefer. Place on the prepared baking tray, cover with a cloth and leave to rest in a warm place for a further 30 minutes.

Meanwhile, preheat the oven to 200°C (fan)/220°C/425°F/Gas mark 7.

Bake the rolls in the oven for about 15 minutes, until golden. Remove from the oven and leave to cool before enjoying.

Spelt is a species of wheat that has been around for thousands of years and was a very important staple in ancient times. As well as its healthy nutritional properties – higher protein content and a good source of fibre – spelt has a delicious nutty flavour which, combined with crunchy walnuts, really comes out in this bread. If you prefer, you can omit the walnuts. This bread is delicious eaten freshly baked with butter or toasted the next day and spread with your favourite jam or honey. *Illustrated overleaf.*

PANE ALLA FARINA DI SPELTA E NOCI
Wholemeal Spelt and Walnut Bread

Serves 6

10g/¼oz fresh yeast
½ tsp runny honey
200ml/7fl oz/scant 1 cup lukewarm water
270g/9½oz/scant 2¼ cups wholemeal
   (wholewheat) spelt flour
3g/just under ⅛oz/½ tsp salt
40g/1½oz/scant ½ cup walnuts, roughly chopped

Line a flat baking tray with parchment paper.

Dissolve the yeast and honey in the lukewarm water. Combine the flour and salt, then add the yeast mixture and mix into a dough. It will be quite sticky but don't worry.

Place the dough on a lightly floured work surface and incorporate the walnuts, kneading for 2 minutes. Shape into a ball, place on the prepared baking tray and, using a sharp knife, make an incision the shape of a cross. Cover with a cloth and leave to rest in a warm place for 1 hour, or until doubled in size.

Preheat the oven to 180°C (fan)/200°C/400°F/Gas mark 6.

Bake in the oven for 45 minutes. Remove from the oven, leave to cool, then slice.

This is a fun bread to make for Halloween! You can make a larger loaf like this one, or smaller individual ones – after the first rising, divide the dough into smaller pieces and follow the recipe as below. I love the combination of pumpkin, chilli and rosemary, but if you prefer you can omit the chilli, especially if making for children. Or, if like me you love chilli, you can add more or less depending on the strength of the chilli.

PANE ALLA ZUCCA
Pumpkin Bread

Makes 8 slices

2 tbsp extra virgin olive oil
2 garlic cloves, squashed
    and left whole
½ red chilli, finely chopped
needles of 1 rosemary
    sprig, finely chopped
200g/7oz pumpkin
    or butternut squash
    (cleaned weight),
    cut into cubes
1 tsp salt
7g/¼oz fresh yeast
80ml/3fl oz/generous ⅓
    cup lukewarm water
350g/12oz/scant 3 cups
    strong white bread flour
1 egg
1 tsp honey
egg wash (see p.13)

Line a flat baking tray with parchment paper.

Heat 1 tablespoon of extra virgin olive oil in a large frying pan, add the garlic, chilli and rosemary and sauté over a medium heat for a minute or so. Stir in the pumpkin or squash and ½ teaspoon salt, then reduce the heat to low, cover with a lid and cook for about 12–15 minutes until the pumpkin has softened. Remove from the heat, leave to cool, discard the garlic, place the pumpkin on a board and roughly chop into smaller pieces. Set aside.

Dissolve the yeast in the lukewarm water. Combine the flour, remaining salt, remaining extra virgin olive oil, the egg, honey and yeast mixture and mix until everything is well incorporated. Place on a floured work surface, add the pumpkin mixture and knead for 10 minutes, adding more flour if you find the dough too sticky. Place in a bowl, cover with clingfilm and leave to rest in a warm place for 2 hours, or until doubled in size.

Knock back the dough on a floured work surface and form into a round ball-type shape, tying with string to make a pumpkin shape (see photo!). Place the dough on the prepared baking tray, brush the top with egg wash and leave in a warm place to rest for a further 1 hour.

Preheat the oven to 180°C (fan)/200°C/400°F/Gas mark 6.

Bake the pumpkin bread in the oven for 30 minutes. Remove from the oven, leave to cool, then tear and share!

Chickpea flour is widely used in Italy when making *farinata*, a type of flatbread sold as street food in Liguria. Combined with gluten-free white flours and yeast, it makes a lovely spongy-textured loaf, and with the addition of mixed seeds it's a very healthy snack to enjoy at any time. It is especially delicious eaten with ham and cheese for a nutritious lunch for anyone on a gluten-free diet. It's also simple and quick to make as it needs to rise only once.

PANE DI FARINA DI CECI E SEMI
Chickpea and Mixed Seed Bread (Gluten-Free)

Serves 4–6

21g/¾oz fresh yeast
10g/¼oz/2 tsp caster (superfine) sugar
215ml/7¼fl oz/scant 1 cup lukewarm water
1 large egg
1 tsp white wine vinegar
15ml/½fl oz/1 tbsp extra virgin olive oil
180g/6½oz/scant 1½ cups white gluten-free flour
  (such as Doves)
80g/3oz/⅔ cup Italian chickpea flour
40g/1½oz mixed seeds, such as pumpkin, sunflower,
  flaxseed and chia
6g/just over ⅛oz/1 tsp salt

Line a 19 x 9cm/7½ x 3½in loaf tin with parchment paper.

Dissolve the yeast and sugar in the lukewarm water. Separately combine the egg, vinegar and extra virgin olive oil.

Combine the flours on a clean work surface, add the egg mixture, then the yeast mixture and stir well. Stir in the seeds and salt until it is all well incorporated. Pour into the prepared tin, cover with clingfilm and leave to rest in a warm place for 1 hour, or until doubled in size.

Preheat the oven to 180°C (fan)/200°C/400°F/Gas mark 6.

Discard the clingfilm and bake the loaf in the oven for 40 minutes. Leave to cool, before turning out of the tin and slicing.

Taralli are an unleavened type of bread snack made into an oval shape originating from Puglia and common all over southern Italy. They date from around the 1400s when they were made by poor people as a bread substitute and have evolved ever since. They are traditionally served by Puglian families when guests visit, with a glass of homemade wine. They can be plain or flavoured with fennel seeds, as below, or other ingredients like black pepper, chilli flakes, herbs, onion and they can also be sweet. These breads make a lovely addition to your bread basket or can be served with drinks or simply enjoyed as a snack at any time. They take time and patience to make, but you could get friends and family involved in rolling and making the little oval shapes; they are well worth it in the end, and they will keep for about a week stored in an airtight container. *Illustrated overleaf.*

TARALLI PUGLIESI
Puglian Bread Snacks

Makes about 70

500g/1lb 2oz/4 cups strong white bread flour
10g/¼oz/1½ tsp salt
1 tsp fennel seeds
125ml/4fl oz/½ cup extra virgin olive oil
200ml/7fl oz/scant 1 cup white wine

Line large baking trays with parchment paper.

Combine the flour, salt and fennel seeds (or other flavouring) on a clean work surface. Add the extra virgin olive oil and wine, and mix into a dough. Knead for about 20 minutes. Form into a ball, wrap in clingfilm and leave to chill for 30 minutes.

Roll a chunk of the dough into a thick sausage shape, then cut out small pieces weighing about 10g/¼oz each. Keep the rest of the dough wrapped in clingfilm to prevent it drying out. Roll out each small piece on a very lightly floured work surface into a thin sausage shape about 10cm/4in in length and close to form an oval shape.

Preheat the oven to 180°C (fan)/200°C/400°F/Gas mark 6.

Bring a large saucepan of water to the boil, drop in a few *taralli* at a time and cook until they rise to the surface. Drain with a slotted spoon and place on a clean tea towel. Leave to dry for 10–15 minutes, then place on the prepared baking tray and bake for 25 minutes until slightly golden.

Remove from the oven, leave to cool, then store in an airtight container.

This savoury cheesy bread originating from Le Marche looks exactly like a *Panettone* (see p.145) with a more spongy texture. It is not clear how this bread came about, but it is traditionally eaten at Eastertime. It is delicious eaten on its own or with a slice of prosciutto.

CRESCIA MARCHIGIANA
Cheesy Panettone

Serves 8–10

25g/1oz fresh yeast
1 tsp caster (superfine) sugar
150ml/5fl oz/⅔ cup lukewarm milk
500g/1lb 2oz/4 cups strong bread flour
150g/5½oz/1⅓ cups grated Parmesan cheese
5 eggs, at room temperature
2 tsp salt
1 tsp black pepper
150ml/5fl oz/⅔ cup extra virgin olive oil
100g/3½oz pecorino cheese, cut into small cubes
a knob of melted butter

Lightly grease a 18cm/7in, 4.5 litre/8 pint *panettone* tin and line with parchment paper.

Dissolve the yeast and sugar in the lukewarm milk.

Combine the flour and grated Parmesan, then gradually add the yeast mixture, mixing well with your hands until it is all well amalgamated. Add the eggs one at a time, mixing well. Season with salt and pepper, then gradually add the extra virgin olive oil and continue to mix. The dough will be sticky but don't worry. If you prefer, you can mix with a wooden spoon or spatula and continue to mix for 10 minutes. Stir in the pecorino and place the mixture into the prepared tin. Brush the top with melted butter and leave to rest in a warm place for 2½ hours, or until the dough has risen to the top of the tin.

Preheat the oven to 180°C (fan)/200°C/400°F/Gas mark 6. Place a small container of water inside one of the corners of the oven.

Bake the *panettone* for 55 minutes. Check by inserting a wooden skewer; if it comes out dry and clean, it is cooked. Remove from the oven, leave to cool slightly, then turn out of the tin, slice and serve.

When I think of bread from Puglia, huge loaves with a thick crust and yellow straw-coloured soft interior come to mind as well as the traditional stone ovens still very much part of the town of Altamura. Altamura, in the province of Bari, has an age-old tradition of bread making and this bread has over time become one of Italy's most renowned breads; it has been given DOP status in the last decade. The bread is made with *semola rimacinata di grano duro* (hard durum wheat semolina) locally grown in the Murgia area and is still made in the traditional method using natural leavens and cooked in wood-fired ovens using oak. Apart from its deliciousness, this bread was and still is made in large loaves of at least 1kg/2lb 4oz in weight and made to last up to a couple of weeks, still reminiscent of the days when farmers had bread and little else to eat during the long hours spent labouring in the fields.

It was quite tricky to recreate this bread at home – it could be the water, yeast, humidity, type of oven – but after many attempts, my wife Liz finally came up with this version of Pane Pugliese. It might not be the same as the Altamura bread, which we eat in Puglia, but it was certainly delicious and the whole loaf disappeared in one evening! You can find the flour in good Italian delis or online. I recommend you make this bread in a freestanding mixer with the kneading attachment as it takes quite a long time to knead by hand – if making by hand then you would need to knead for about 40 minutes.

PANE PUGLIESE
Puglian Bread

Serves 6

7g/¼oz fresh yeast
315ml/10½fl oz/scant 1½ cups lukewarm water
450g/15oz/scant 2⅓ cups hard durum wheat
    semolina (*semola rimacinata di grano duro*) flour
80g/3oz *biga* made with semolina (see p.13)
8g/¼oz/1¼ tsp salt

Sprinkle a flat baking tray with flour.

Dissolve the yeast in the lukewarm water. Place the flour in a freestanding mixer, add the *biga*, switch the machine on the lowest setting and mix for a minute or so. With the machine still on, gradually add the yeast mixture and mix for 2 minutes. Add the salt and continue to mix for 20 minutes.

Remove the dough from the mixer and place in a bowl, cover with clingfilm, and leave to rest in a warm place for 2 hours.

Place the dough on a lightly floured work surface and knock back gently with a couple of folds. Shape into a long or round loaf. Make incisions

with a sharp knife, sprinkle some flour all over the dough, then place on the prepared tray and leave to rest in a warm place for 30 minutes.

Meanwhile, preheat the oven at 220°C (fan)/240°C/475°F/Gas mark 9.

Bake the bread in the oven for 25 minutes. Remove from the oven and leave to cool before slicing.

This savoury version of the sweet Austrian-inspired brioche cake is truly scrumptious. In Naples, where it is commonly eaten, it is traditionally filled with pieces of salami and local cheese. You can fill it with anything you like and I have given you a few ideas. You can stick to one filling or, to make it more interesting, you can fill each ball with something different! Perfect for tearing and sharing and seeing who gets what! It's delicious as a nutritious snack at any time or for putting in lunch boxes. Check out the sweet version on p.148.

DANUBIO SALATO
Savoury Brioche

Serves 4–6

6g/just over ⅛oz fresh yeast
115ml/4fl oz/½ cup lukewarm milk
275g/9¾oz/scant 2¼ cups strong white bread flour
15g/½oz/1 tbsp caster (superfine) sugar
1 tsp salt
1 egg, beaten
50ml/2fl oz/scant ¼ cup extra virgin olive oil
egg wash (see p.13)
FOR THE FILLING:
mortadella, cheese, salami, grilled preserved
    vegetables, pesto, sun-dried tomatoes

Dissolve the yeast in the lukewarm milk. Combine the flour, sugar and salt on a clean work surface. Add the yeast mixture and mix until it is well amalgamated. Add the egg, extra virgin olive oil and mix together into a soft dough. Knead for about 10 minutes. Cover with clingfilm and leave to rest in a warm place for 2 hours, or until doubled in size.

Meanwhile, prepare your fillings and line a 20cm/8in round cake tin with parchment paper.

Divide the dough into 15 pieces, about 30g/1oz each. Shape each piece into balls and, using a rolling pin, flatten them into small circles on a lightly floured work surface. Place a little filling of your choice in the centre of each circle and close the edges well to form small balls. Place in the prepared tin, cover with clingfilm and rest for a further 1 hour.

Preheat the oven to 160°C (fan)/180°C/350°F/Gas mark 4.

Brush egg wash all over the top of the brioche and bake in the oven for 25 minutes until golden brown. Remove from the oven, leave to cool slightly, then tear and share.

This deliciously moist and aromatic tomato loaf is more like a savoury cake, hence the absence of yeast and no proving time. I urge you to use good-quality preserved sun-dried tomatoes – if necessary, buy the dried ones and marinate them yourself with olive oil, garlic, dried oregano and some chilli for a couple of days in a sealed container before using. This loaf makes a wonderful addition to your bread basket or you can eat it on its own as a snack. It also looks very pretty!

PANE AI POMODORI
Tomato Loaf

Serves 4–6

125g/4½oz/1 cup plain (all-purpose) flour
7g/¼oz/1¾ tsp baking powder
45g/1½oz/generous ⅓ cup grated Parmesan
    cheese, plus extra for sprinkling
1 tsp fennel seeds
3 eggs
40g/1½oz/3 tbsp melted butter, cooled
2 tbsp double (heavy) cream
50g/1¾oz sun-dried tomatoes, finely chopped
salt
½ tsp black pepper
handful of basil leaves
120g/4oz baby tomatoes, leave the stalks on a few

Preheat the oven to 180°C (fan)/200°C/400°F/Gas mark 6 and line a 19 x 9cm/7½ x 3½in loaf tin with parchment paper.

Combine the flour, baking powder, grated Parmesan and fennel seeds and set aside.

Whisk the eggs, melted butter and cream together in a large bowl until well combined and creamy. Stir in the sun-dried tomatoes. Fold in the flour mixture and mix with a spoon until it is all well incorporated. Stir in a little salt (careful, sun-dried tomatoes can be quite salty), black pepper and basil leaves. Pour the mixture into the prepared loaf tin. Push a few baby tomatoes into the mixture, sprinkle a little grated Parmesan over, and place the tomatoes with stalks on top, pressing slightly, for decoration.

Cover with foil and bake in the oven for 30 minutes. Remove the foil and bake for a further 10 minutes until golden. Check by inserting a wooden skewer as you would for a cake; if it comes out clean, it is ready. Remove from the oven, leave to cool, then remove from the tin, slice and serve.

FOCACCIA

Focaccia has age-old roots; it is believed it first came about as an unleavened flatbread, which bakers would rustle up and bake on the bottom of the oven so they could have something nourishing to see them through the long night shift.

The Latin for focaccia is *focacius*, meaning hearth or fireplace. The Romans made a type of focaccia using flour, salt, yeast, extra virgin olive oil and water, cooking it on the hearth and using it as bread to dip into soup.

Focaccia, as we know it today, originated in the northwestern region of Liguria: the two main varieties are the *fugassa*, sometimes known as *schiacciata*, from Genova – the classic dimpled flatbread with extra virgin olive oil and salt; the other, from the town of Recco, is made with oozing soft cheese in the middle.

Legend tells us that Ligurian focaccia started off as a survival food during the Saracen invasions – people would flee the coast seeking refuge inland and using ingredients they could find to cook with, like flour, water, extra virgin olive oil and local soft cheese. By combining these few simple ingredients, a type of focaccia was made. This story has eventually led to making the *Focaccia al formaggio di Recco* a trademark, with strict guidelines on the type of ingredients used and how it should be made for it to be recognised as authentic.

In Liguria, focaccia is a popular street food and stalls selling *fugassa* (local dialect) are many. Locals even eat focaccia for breakfast, dipping it into their cappuccino.

In the rest of Italy, focaccia is often a term loosely applied to all sorts of baked goods both savoury and sweet. I remember as child growing up in southern Italy my mum would often ask me to pick up a sweet focaccia from the bakery, which was like a sweet bread type of cake and nothing to do with an oily flatbread. In other parts too, focaccia can mean a totally different item – in Lucania, a pepper bread is known as a focaccia called *Strazzata* (see p.70). And in Puglia, they make one stuffed and rolled – *Focaccia Arrotolata* (see p.65). In Sicily, a round focaccia is made topped with a tomato and anchovy sauce known as *Sfincione*.

The focaccia I make is a cross between pizza and bread, as I make it thicker than a pizza but with similar toppings. The classic indentations made before rising are so the extra virgin olive oil can penetrate the dough, giving it that oily focaccia taste and texture. Toppings vary from simply salt and herbs to more substantial ingredients like potatoes, onions or peppers. Like pizza, a focaccia can be topped with almost anything you like. It is often served as a substitute to bread during meal times or can be filled with cured meats and enjoyed as a snack or for a packed lunch. Leftover focaccia is delicious reheated in the oven the next day.

I first developed this 'deep-pan' focaccia recipe many years ago for Antonio Carluccio's restaurant – it was a hit, and I eventually experimented with different toppings. It is lovely sliced in half and filled with prosciutto or other cured meats or cheese or even grilled vegetables for a delicious sandwich. Focaccia is best eaten on the day it is baked, but it will keep for a few days and you can freshen it up in the oven for a few minutes before serving.

FOCACCIA AL SALE
Basic Focaccia with Sea Salt

Serves 6–8

FOR THE DOUGH:
12g/just under ½oz fresh yeast
350ml/12fl oz/1½ cups lukewarm water
500g/1lb 2oz/4 cups strong white bread flour
2 tsp salt
semolina or dried breadcrumbs, for sprinkling
FOR THE TOPPING:
1 tbsp extra virgin olive oil, plus extra for drizzling
1 tsp Maldon sea salt
freshly ground black pepper

Dissolve the yeast in the warm water. Place the flour and salt on a clean work surface, add the yeast mixture and mix to form a soft dough. Lightly flour the work surface and knead well for 5 minutes until smooth and elastic. Cover with a tea towel and rest in a warm place for 20 minutes.

Preheat the oven to 220°C (fan)/240°C/475°F/Gas mark 9.

Roll the dough out on a lightly floured work surface to a rectangular shape roughly the same as the baking tin, either 37.5 x 28cm/14¾ x 11in or a large round tin, about 37cm/14½in in diameter (as in the photo). Warm the baking tin in the oven for about 10 seconds, then remove and lightly sprinkle with some semolina or breadcrumbs. Place the rolled-out dough in the tin and pour the olive oil in the middle. Using your fingers, spread the olive oil all over the dough. Leave for 5 minutes, then poke the dough all over with your fingers to make indentations. Sprinkle all over with salt and a little black pepper. Cover with a cloth and leave to rest in a warm place for 45 minutes, or until doubled in size.

Bake for about 20 minutes until evenly golden brown. Check the focaccia occasionally as domestic ovens often colour one side more, so turn the baking tray round accordingly. Once cooked, remove from the oven and drizzle a little olive oil all over. Leave to cool, then cut into squares.

This uses the same method as the Basic Focaccia (see p.56) with the addition of garlic and rosemary to give it an extra kick. Like the Basic Focaccia, this is ideal to slice and fill as sandwiches or add to your bread basket for a delicious alternative, especially when serving a selection of cured meats as an antipasto. I love the way the rosemary goes crispy in the oven!

FOCACCIA CON AGLIO E ROSMARINO
Focaccia with Garlic and Rosemary

Serves 6–8

FOR THE DOUGH:
1 quantity of Basic Focaccia (see p.56)
semolina or breadcrumbs, for sprinkling
FOR THE TOPPING:
1 tbsp extra virgin olive oil, plus extra for drizzling
2 garlic cloves, finely chopped
needles of 2 rosemary branches, finely chopped
1 tsp Maldon sea salt
freshly ground black pepper

Make the dough according to the recipe on p.56.

Preheat the oven to 220°C (fan)/240°C/475°F/Gas mark 9.

Roll out the dough on a lightly floured work surface into a rectangular shape roughly the same as a 37.5 x 28cm/14¾ x 11in baking tray. Warm the baking tin in the oven for about 10 seconds, then remove and sprinkle with some semolina or breadcrumbs. Place the rolled-out dough in the tray and pour the extra virgin olive oil in the middle. With your fingers, spread the oil all over the dough. Leave for 5 minutes, then poke the dough all over with your fingers to make indentations. Sprinkle the garlic, rosemary, salt and a little black pepper over the top. Cover with a cloth and leave to rest in a warm place for 45 minutes, or until doubled in size.

Bake the focaccia in the oven for about 15 minutes until evenly golden brown. Check the focaccia occasionally as domestic ovens often colour one side more, so turn the baking tray round accordingly.

Once cooked, remove from the oven and immediately drizzle a little extra virgin olive oil all over. Leave to cool, then cut into squares.

This delicious cheesy focaccia dates back to the days of the Saracen invasions when people fled the coast to the safety inland where only basic ingredients were available like flour, oil and cheese. Hence the birth of this renowned focaccia so popular in the Ligurian region where it is sold everywhere. The cheese used is normally a local soft cheese, or *stracchino* is popular. My version has *Dolcelatte*, which gives a more pungent flavour.

FOCACCIA LIGURE AL FORMAGGIO
Ligurian Cheese Focaccia

Serves 6–8

12g/just under ½oz fresh yeast
250ml/9fl oz/generous 1 cup lukewarm water
500g/1lb 2oz/4 cups strong white bread flour
6g/¼oz/1 tsp salt
3 tbsp extra virgin olive oil, plus extra for brushing
250g/9oz Dolcelatte cheese, roughly chopped
freshly ground black pepper

Dissolve the yeast in the lukewarm water. Place the flour and salt on a clean work surface, add the yeast mixture and olive oil, and gradually mix to form a dough. Knead for about 10 minutes until smooth and elastic. Place in a large bowl, cover with clingfilm and leave to rest in a warm place for 1 hour, or until doubled in size.

Preheat the oven to 200°C (fan)/220°C/425°F/Gas mark 7. Grease a rectangular baking tray, about 33 x 30cm/13 x 12in with a little extra virgin olive oil.

Divide the dough in half. Roll out one piece into a roughly rectangular shape, stretching by hand until it is 3mm/⅛in thick. Line the prepared baking tin with the dough. Place pieces of cheese all over and sprinkle with salt and pepper.

Roll out the other piece of dough to the same thickness. Place over the cheese, pressing down well with your fingertips and sealing the edges well so none of the filling can escape. Brush olive oil all over the top and bake in the oven for about 20–25 minutes until golden.

Remove from the oven and leave to rest for a couple of minutes, then slice and enjoy!

This focaccia is made the same way as the Basic Focaccia (see p.56) with the addition of peppers and olives as a topping. I love *agrodolce* of peppers – red and yellow peppers cooked in sugar and vinegar to give it a slightly sweet and sour flavour. *Agrodolce* of peppers is much better made the day before and stored in the refrigerator overnight so all the flavours can infuse nicely before using it to top the focaccia. Sometimes when I make lots of *agrodolce*, this is how I use up the leftovers.

FOCACCIA CON AGRODOLCE DI PEPERONI
Focaccia with Peppers

Serves 6–8

1 quantity of Basic Focaccia
  (see p.56)
FOR THE TOPPING:
3 tbsp extra virgin olive oil,
  plus extra for drizzling
1 red (bell) pepper, sliced
  into thick strips
1 yellow (bell) pepper,
  sliced into thick strips
1 garlic clove, left whole
6 pitted black olives
6 pitted green olives
½ tbsp capers
½ tbsp granulated sugar
2 tbsp white wine vinegar
salt and freshly ground
  black pepper
6 basil leaves

First, make the *agrodolce* of peppers. Heat 2 tablespoons of the extra virgin olive oil in a large frying pan, add the peppers and cook over a high-medium heat for 5 minutes, or until the skins are golden brown, stirring from time to time. Add the garlic, olives and capers, stir in the sugar, add the vinegar and allow to evaporate, about 1 minute. Reduce the heat slightly and cook over a medium heat for about 5 minutes until the peppers are cooked through but not mushy. Season to taste with salt and pepper and stir in the basil leaves. Set aside or, if you are making the day before, cover and leave to chill until required.

Preheat the oven to 220°C (fan)/240°C/475°F/Gas mark 9.

Make the Basic Focaccia dough according to the recipe on p.56, but do not add the salt at the end. Warm the baking tray in the oven for about 10 seconds, then remove and sprinkle with some semolina or breadcrumbs. Place the rolled-out dough in the tray and pour the remaining extra virgin olive oil in the middle. Using your fingers, spread the olive oil all over the dough. Leave for 5 minutes, then poke the dough all over with your fingers to make indentations. Top the focaccia with the mixture of peppers. Cover with a cloth and leave to rest in a warm place for 45 minutes.

Bake in the oven for 15–20 minutes until evenly golden. Check it occasionally as domestic ovens often colour one side more, so turn the baking tray round accordingly.

Remove from the oven and immediately drizzle a little extra virgin olive oil all over. Leave to cool, then slice into squares.

The addition of mashed potatoes to focaccia dough is so typical of Puglia. To make it go further, a rich filling of eggs, cured meats and cheese is often added and the focaccia is rolled up. In this recipe, raw beaten eggs are included which are gently cooked while baking. Once cooked and cooled, slices are cut and the end result is like a delicious *panino*, which is a meal in itself. It is ideal to take on picnics or for packed lunches. If wrapped in foil or clingfilm, it can be kept for a couple of days.

FOCACCIA ARROTOLATA PUGLIESE
Rolled and Filled Pugliese Focaccia

Serves 10

FOR THE DOUGH:
280g/10oz floury (mealy)
   potatoes, unpeeled
25g/1oz fresh yeast
200ml/7fl oz/scant 1 cup
   lukewarm water
500g/1lb 2oz/4 cups
   strong white bread flourr
8g/scant ¼oz/1½ tsp salt
extra virgin olive oil,
   for brushing
FOR THE FILLING:
3 eggs
100g/3½oz/scant 1 cup
   grated Parmesan cheese
2 balls of mozzarella, sliced
175g/6oz good-quality
   Italian skinless sausages,
   roughly chopped
120g/4oz cooked ham
   (about 5 thin slices)

Line a large flat baking tray with parchment paper.

Cook the whole potatoes until tender, then drain well, return to the pan and mash. Leave to cool.

Dissolve the yeast in the lukewarm water. Mix the flour and salt together on a clean work surface, add the mashed potato and gradually add the yeast mixture, mixing well to form a dough. Knead for 10 minutes, then form into a ball. Place a clean large tea towel on the work surface lightly dusted with flour. Place the dough on top and, using a rolling pin, roll out to a roughly rectangular shape about 4mm/⅛in thick. Brush all over with a little olive oil.

Whisk the eggs and Parmesan together in a small bowl, then spread this mixture over the dough, leaving a border all round of about 2cm/¾in. Scatter pieces of mozzarella and sausage over the top, then add slices of ham. Brush lightly with a little more oil.

Roll into a big fat sausage, making sure all the filling is tucked inside and the edges are well sealed. With the help of the tea towel, carefully place the rolled focaccia onto the prepared tray, making sure you place the seam on the bottom. Cover and leave to rest in a warm place for 2 hours, or until doubled in size.

Preheat the oven to 180°C (fan)/200°C/400°F/Gas mark 6.

Brush the top of the focaccia with a little olive oil and bake in the oven for 45 minutes. Remove from the oven and leave to cool for 10 minutes before eating.

This is made the same way as the Basic Focaccia (p.56), but with the addition of a delicious and substantial topping. The lightly roasted potatoes, pancetta, onion and sage marry well together to make this focaccia a meal in itself. It is ideal for a packed lunch or a picnic.

FOCACCIA CON PATATE, CIPOLLE ROSSE E PANCETTA

Focaccia with Potato, Red Onion and Pancetta

Serves 6–8

1 quantity of Basic Focaccia
   (see p.56)
FOR THE TOPPING:
2 tbsp extra virgin olive oil,
   plus extra for drizzling
300g/10½oz potatoes,
   peeled and sliced into
   1cm/½in rounds
salt and freshly ground
   black pepper
8 sage leaves
75g/2¾oz pancetta, diced
1 medium red onion, sliced
a little semolina or
   dried breadcrumbs,
   for sprinkling

Preheat the oven to 220°C (fan)/240°C/475°F/Gas mark 9. Lightly grease a flat baking tray.

Place the potato rounds on the prepared baking tray, sprinkle with some salt and pepper and a little drizzle of extra virgin olive oil, and roast in the oven for about 10 minutes until golden and cooked through. Remove from the oven and set aside.

Heat the 2 tablespoons extra virgin olive oil in a small frying pan, add 2 sage leaves, the onion and pancetta, and sauté for 4 minutes, or until soft. Remove from the heat and set aside.

Make the basic focaccia dough according to the recipe on p.56, but do not add salt at the end. After spreading over the extra virgin olive oil and making indentations all over the dough, arrange the potatoes, onions, pancetta and remaining sage leaves on top. Cover with a cloth and rest in a warm place for 45 minutes, or until doubled in size.

Preheat the oven to 200°C (fan)/220°C/425°F/Gas Mark 7.

Bake in the oven for about 20 minutes until evenly golden around the edges. Remove from the oven, immediately drizzle with a little extra virgin olive oil, leave to cool, then slice into squares.

This Ligurian speciality has age-old roots and legend tells us that it was made for the Genovese Admiral, Andrea Doria, hence the name. Because of the border between Liguria and France, this focaccia is also popular in the Provence region where it is known as *pissaladiere*. Over time, tomatoes have been added to this dish, making it like a *Napoletana* pizza topping, but I like this original version with onion and anchovies. I like to make mine in a square, but you can make it round, rectangular or any shape you prefer. Cut into slices and serve as part of a meal when you have a crowd or simply enjoy as a snack at any time. It's delicious enjoyed hot or cold. *Illustrated overleaf.*

PISCIALANDREA DI IMPERIA
Onion and Anchovy Focaccia

Serves 6

FOR THE DOUGH:
10g/¼oz fresh yeast
300ml/10fl oz/1¼ cups
    lukewarm water
500g/1lb 2oz/4 cups
    strong white bread flour
6g/just over ⅛oz/1 tsp salt
20ml/¾fl oz/4 tsp extra
    virgin olive oil
plain (all-purpose) flour or
    dried breadcrumbs,
    for sprinkling
FOR THE TOPPING:
3 tbsp extra virgin olive oil
2 medium red onions,
    finely chopped
about 18 anchovy fillets
20 pitted black olives
1 tsp dried oregano

Dissolve the yeast in the lukewarm water. Mix the flour and salt together in a large bowl, add the extra virgin olive oil and yeast mixture and mix to form a dough. Knead the dough for 10 minutes, form into a ball, cover with clingfilm and leave to rest for 30 minutes, or until doubled in size.

Divide the dough in half and knead each piece for 2 minutes. Shape into balls, cover with a damp cloth and leave to rest for a further 30 minutes, or until doubled in size.

Preheat the oven to 220°C (fan)/240°C/475°F/Gas mark 9 and sprinkle 2 flat square 30 x 30cm/12 x 12in baking trays or 2 x round flat 30cm/12in baking trays with a little flour or dried breadcrumbs.

Meanwhile, prepare the topping. Heat the extra virgin olive oil in a frying pan, add 2 anchovy fillets and dissolve. Add the onion and cook over a low heat for 8–10 minutes, or until softened. Remove and set aside.

Place one ball of dough onto a slightly floured work surface and, using your fingers, spread into your preferred baking tray. Repeat with the other piece of dough. Top with the onion mixture, arrange the remaining anchovy fillets and black olives and sprinkle with dried oregano. Bake in the oven for about 20 minutes until the edges are golden.

Although it looks very much like a ring-shaped bread, it is locally known as 'focaccia'. It can only be found in the rural Lucania area of Basilicata in southern Italy and was traditionally made for wedding ceremonies to be eaten with ham, cheese and preserved vegetables and enjoyed with wine. In local dialect *strazzata* means to tear with your hands, which is how this pepper-based focaccia was always eaten, and the more pepper it contained the more wine would be consumed at the wedding feast. Locals are very proud of this speciality and even hold annual festivals in its honour.

STRAZZATA LUCANA
Pepper Ring Focaccia

Serves 10–12

15g/½oz fresh yeast
320ml/10¾fl oz/scant 1½ cups lukewarm water
250g/9oz/2 cups strong white bread flour
250g/9oz/scant 1½ cups cups semolina flour
   (*grano duro*)
2g/¼ tsp salt
15g/½oz/1 tbsp black pepper

Line a large flat baking tray with parchment paper.

Dissolve the yeast in the lukewarm water.

Mix the flours, salt and black pepper together. Add the yeast mixture and mix to form a dough. Knead for 10 minutes, cover with clingfilm and leave to rest in a warm place for 1 hour, or until doubled in size.

Roll out the dough on a lightly floured work surface into a long sausage shape about 63cm/25in in length, flatten lightly with your hands, then form into a ring. You may want to place a foil-covered small bowl in the centre so the bread stays in a ring shape. Place on the prepared baking tray, cover with a cloth and leave to rest in a warm place for 1 hour.

Preheat the oven to 220°C (fan)/240°C/475°F/Gas mark 9.

Bake the *strazzata* in the oven for 15 minutes, or until golden brown.

Remove from the oven, leave to cool, then serve.

It's quite common in Italy, especially in rural wine-making areas, to set aside some grapes to make into bread or focaccia or like these buns. I remember at grape harvest time, the baker in our village would make something like this with leftover bread dough. The addition of cinnamon and rosemary really enhance the flavour of the grapes and dough. It's delicious at teatime!

RONDELLE ALL'UVA E ROSMARINO
Grape and Rosemary Buns

Makes 10–12 buns

300g/10½oz grapes, halved
15ml/½fl oz/1 tbsp white wine
20g/¾oz/7 tsp light soft brown sugar
grated zest of ½ lemon
1 tsp ground cinnamon
12g/just under ½oz fresh yeast
160ml/5½fl oz/¾ cup lukewarm milk
350g/12oz/1½ cups strong white bread flour
needles of 1 rosemary sprig
a little extra virgin olive oil, for brushing

Line a large flat baking tray with parchment paper.

Place the grapes, wine, sugar, lemon zest and cinnamon in a small bowl and leave to macerate.

Dissolve the yeast in the milk. Place the flour in a large bowl and gradually add the yeast mixture to mix into a dough. Place the dough on a lightly floured work surface and knead for 10 minutes, then form into a ball, cover with clingfilm and leave to rest in a warm place for 15 minutes.

Roll out the dough into a rectangular shape. Scatter the grapes all over followed by the rosemary needles. Roll the dough into a long thick sausage and carefully cut out 2.5cm/1in chunks. The grapes may escape but press them back in and form the dough into little basket shapes. Place on the prepared baking tray, brush with a little extra virgin olive oil, cover with a cloth, and leave to rest in a warm place for 30 minutes.

Preheat the oven to 200°C (fan)/220°C/425°F/Gas mark 7.

Bake the buns in the oven for 15 minutes until golden brown. Remove from the oven, leave to cool and enjoy!

I love sun-dried tomatoes but the ones that you buy here are not always the same flavoursome ones I am used to in Italy. So I like to marinate them myself before eating or using them in my recipes, such as this one to top focaccia.

FOCACCIA CON POMODORI SECCHI
Focaccia with Sun-Dried Tomatoes

Serves 6–8

FOR THE DOUGH:
1 quantity of Basic Focaccia
  (see p.56)
semolina or dried
  breadcrumbs, for dusting
FOR THE TOPPING:
100g/3½oz preserved
  sun-dried tomatoes
  in oil (weight with oil
  drained off)
2 garlic cloves, whole
1 tsp dried chilli (red
  pepper) flakes
1 tsp dried oregano
12 basil leaves
1 tbsp extra virgin olive oil,
  plus extra for drizzling

First prepare the sun-dried tomatoes. Remove the tomatoes from the jar and place in a bowl, reserving the oil. Add the garlic, chilli, oregano and basil, then place in an airtight container. Pour a little of the oil from the jar, just enough to cover the tomatoes, cover with a lid and leave overnight to marinate.

Make the focaccia according to the recipe on p.56.

Preheat the oven to 220°C (fan)/240°C/475°F/Gas mark 9.

Roll the dough out on a lightly floured work surface to a rectangular shape roughly the same as the baking tin, either 37.5 x 28cm/14¾ x 11in or a large round baking tin, about 37cm/14½in in diameter.

Warm the baking tin in the oven for about 10 seconds, then remove and sprinkle with some semolina or breadcrumbs. Place the rolled-out dough in the tray and pour the extra virgin olive oil in the middle. Using your fingers, spread the olive oil all over the dough. Leave for 5 minutes, then poke the dough all over with your fingers to make indentations, then top the focaccia with the sun-dried tomato mixture. Cover with a cloth and leave to rest in a warm place for 45 minutes.

Bake the focaccia in the oven for about 20 minutes until evenly golden brown. Check the focaccia occasionally as domestic ovens often colour one side more, so turn the baking tray round accordingly.

Remove from the oven and immediately drizzle a little olive oil all over. Leave to cool, then cut into squares.

This lovely sweet focaccia is ideal at teatime or even for breakfast. I have made it with plums, but you can substitute with seasonal fruit like peaches, apricots, apples, pears or figs. I like to drizzle a little honey over the top and enjoy it with a coffee. The sweetness comes from the fruit and honey as only a very small amount of sugar is sprinkled so it is a healthy treat. You could enjoy it alongside some soft cheese like creamy *Dolcelatte*, especially if making with figs.

FOCACCIA DOLCE CON LA FRUTTA
Sweet Focaccia with Fruit

Serves 4–6

10g/¼oz fresh yeast
200ml/7fl oz/scant 1 cup
    lukewarm water
350g/12oz/scant 3 cups
    strong white bread flour
4g/scant ⅛oz/½ tsp salt
20ml/¾fl oz/4 tsp extra
    virgin olive oil,
    plus extra for drizzling
1 tbsp runny honey, plus
    extra for drizzling
3 plums or other fruit
1 tbsp water
20ml/¾fl oz/4 tsp Marsala
    or other sweet wine
extra virgin olive oil,
    for drizzling
a little caster (superfine)
    sugar, for sprinkling
a little sifted icing
    (confectioners') sugar,
    for sprinkling

Lightly grease a rectangular shallow roasting-type tin, about 26 x 17cm/10½ x 6½in with extra virgin olive oil.

Dissolve the yeast in the lukewarm water.

Mix the flour, salt, olive oil and honey together. Add the yeast mixture and mix into a dough. Knead for 10 minutes to form a smooth dough. Cover with clingfilm and leave to rest in a warm place for about 1 hour, or until doubled in size.

Meanwhile, slice the plums or other fruit into segments and place in a bowl with the water and Marsala or other sweet wine to macerate.

Place the dough in the prepared tin, drizzle with extra virgin olive oil, and with your fingers make indentations all over. Drain the plums and arrange on top of the dough, then sprinkle with a little sugar. Leave to rest in a warm place for 30 minutes, or until doubled in size.

Preheat the oven to 170°C (fan)/190°C/375°F/Gas mark 5.

Bake in the oven for about 15 minutes until golden round the edges. Remove, sprinkle with icing sugar and place under a hot grill for 2 minutes until caramelised.

Remove from the oven, leave to cool, then slice and serve drizzled with a little runny honey, if liked.

PIZZE

The humble pizza has certainly conquered the world and can be found almost everywhere nowadays wherever you might be.

This simple dough-based treat topped with all sorts of delicious ingredients is loved by all – kids and adults alike – always a favourite for an informal evening out, children's parties, as well as street food or quite simply to enjoy at home.

The origins of pizza are not known for certain, except that it originated as street food in Naples. In fact, it probably started as a type of flatbread, which bakers used to test the heat of the oven before baking the daily loaves. To add a little flavour, the bakers would top the flatbreads with some lard, salt, garlic and herbs. With the introduction of tomatoes in the 1700s, this street food for the poor evolved. It was also a great way for housewives to use up bits of leftovers and top bread dough to make the meal go further.

A century later, a Neapolitan pizza maker created a pizza for Queen Margherita using ingredients of the same colour as the Italian flag for its topping – tomatoes, mozzarella, basil. The Queen loved it, the combination had been a success and that is apparently how Pizza Margherita came about. Whether this story is true or not, Pizza Margherita is still made and loved the world over and its ingredients used as a basic topping for many other pizzas.

Over the years, pizza has evolved not only with toppings but also with shapes like *Calzone* (see p109), which is basically a folded-over pizza, and *Saltimbocca* (see p.106) whose pizza dough balloons out during baking and is then filled.

Street food pizza in Italy is commonly sold *al taglio*, by the slice. In pizzerias, it is sometimes served *al metro*, by the metre – long rectangular-shaped pizzas are placed in the middle of the table with different toppings so everyone gets to try a variety – really fun to do when there is a group of you. *Pizzette* or small pizzas (see pp.94–104) are found in bakeries and snack bars and are ideal as food on the go.

As with any popular dish, it will inevitably be badly copied. And pizza is no exception; there are so many poorly made versions, whether sold in restaurants, takeaways or the ready-made shop-bought variety, that it makes me wonder why such a simple dish can be made so badly. Of course, there is nothing nicer than making your own pizza from scratch – it's so simple and economical, it seems mad not to. Pizza dough can be made in advance and left in the refrigerator, or even frozen and used when required. See overleaf for some of my tips when making pizza at home.

TIPS FOR MAKING PIZZA:

• Knead the dough well so it becomes elastic and smooth.

• Make the base as thin as you can.

• Use tomato passata instead of canned tomatoes as this is ready-sieved.

• Beware of adding too much tomato sauce as this will make the pizza soggy.

• Drizzle a little extra virgin olive oil over the base and topping to help it crisp up.

• Ensure the oven is hot and reaches its temperature before baking the pizza.

BASIC PIZZA DOUGH

Makes 2 round pizzas,
   about 32cm/12½in in diameter,
   or 3 thinner bases,
   as used for Pizza Bianca recipes (p.82)

10g/¼oz fresh yeast
325ml/11fl oz/scant 1½ cups lukewarm water
500g/1lb 2oz/4 cups strong white bread flour
2 tsp salt

Lightly flour a flat baking tray.

Dissolve the yeast in the lukewarm water.

Mix the flour and salt together on a clean work surface, then gradually stir in the yeast mixture to make a dough. Knead the dough for 10 minutes, cover with a cloth and leave to rest for 10 minutes.

Divide the dough into the required number of pieces and knead each for 2 minutes. Place on the prepared baking tray, cover with a cloth and leave to rise in a warm place for 1 hour, or until doubled in size.

Use according to your recipe.

Pizza bianca is a plain pizza, which I like to top lightly with a little sea salt and some extra virgin olive oil, but if you prefer you can just leave it completely plain or add other flavours such as herbs and chilli. It is often served instead of bread with antipasto dishes. Make sure you get the pizza dough as thin as you can so it crisps up a bit during baking.

PIZZA BIANCA

Makes 3 round pizzas,
about 32cm/12½in in diameter

1 quantity of Basic Pizza Dough (see p.80)
coarse sea salt and freshly ground black pepper
extra virgin olive oil

Make the dough according to the recipe on p.80. Lightly flour 3 large flat baking trays.

Divide the dough into 3 equal pieces and knead each for 2 minutes. Place each on a prepared baking tray, cover with a cloth and leave to rise in a warm place for 1 hour, or until doubled in size.

Preheat the oven to 220°C (fan)/240°C/475°F/Gas mark 9.

Roll out each piece of dough on a lightly floured work surface as thinly as you can into a circle. Place on the prepared baking trays and sprinkle each pizza base with some salt and pepper and a drizzle of extra virgin olive oil or with the toppings below.

Bake in the oven for about 10 minutes.

OTHER TOPPINGS:
Grated Parmesan cheese and sage leaves
Olive oil and sliced red chilli

Marinara is a traditional pizza topping in Naples with tomatoes, garlic and anchovies without using any cheese. To give this pizza a twist and make it visually appealing, I have used a variety of coloured tomatoes readily available in shops and markets these days. It's perfect to make during late summer when local tomato varieties are in abundance.

PIZZA MARINARA
Pizza with Mixed Tomatoes and Anchovies

Makes 2 round 32cm/12½in in diameter pizzas

1 quantity of Basic Pizza Dough (see p.80)
FOR THE TOPPING:
350g/12oz mixed yellow, orange and red cherry tomatoes
2 garlic cloves, finely chopped
4 tbsp extra virgin olive oil, plus extra for drizzling
8 anchovy fillets
10 black olives, halved
½ red chilli, finely chopped (optional)
pinch of dried oregano
handful of basil leaves

Make the pizza dough according to the recipe on p.80. Lightly flour a large flat baking tray.

Divide the dough into 2 equal pieces and knead each for 2 minutes. Place on the prepared baking tray, cover with a cloth and leave to rise for 1 hour, or until doubled in size.

Preheat the oven to 220°C (fan)/240°C/475°F/Gas mark 9.

Combine all the topping ingredients together and leave to marinate for about 30 minutes. Top each pizza base with the tomato mixture and bake in the oven for about 10 minutes.

Remove from the oven, drizzle with a little extra virgin olive oil and serve immediately.

I love this classic pizza with bubbly cheesy deliciousness. You can substitute the cheeses with others if you prefer, such as *Dolcelatte*, pecorino or even a hard mozzarella or *ricotta salata*. Go easy on the salt as certain cheeses are quite salty. It's perfect to enjoy with a refreshing glass of beer! .

PIZZA AI 4 FORMAGGI
Pizza Topped with 4 Cheeses

Makes 2 round pizzas,
about 32cm/12½in in diameter

1 quantity of Basic Pizza Dough (see p.80)
FOR THE TOPPING:
extra virgin olive oil, for drizzling
50g/1¾oz Gorgonzola cheese, roughly chopped
50g/1¾oz fontina cheese, roughly chopped
50g/1¾oz provolone (or mature Cheddar) cheese,
   roughly chopped
50g/1¾oz grated Parmesan cheese
salt and freshly ground black pepper

Make the dough according to the recipe on p.80. Lightly flour a flat baking tray.

Divide the dough into half and knead each piece for 2 minutes. Place on the prepared baking tray, cover with a cloth and leave to rise for 1 hour, or until doubled in size.

Preheat the oven to 220°C (fan)/240°C/475°F/Gas mark 9.

Spread a little extra virgin olive oil over each pizza base, top with the cheeses, sprinkle with salt and pepper to taste and add a little drizzle of olive oil.

Bake in the oven for about 10 minutes until the cheeses melt and bubble.

Although I don't normally cook the tomato before topping a pizza, I make an exception with this particular sauce. I love making it when I have an abundance of tomatoes – so simple – just bake tomatoes in the oven with seasoning and the flavours will infuse beautifully, giving you a rich and flavoursome sauce. I suggest you make lots and any leftover sauce can be used to dress pasta, or it is simply delicious on toast or with some bread.

PIZZA CON SALSA DI POMODORINI AL FORNO
Pizza Topped with Oven-Baked Tomato Sauce

Makes 2 round pizzas, 32cm/12½in in diameter

1 quantity of Basic Pizza Dough (see p.80)
FOR THE TOPPING:
600g/1lb 5oz baby plum tomatoes, sliced in half
4 tbsp extra virgin olive oil, plus extra for drizzling
3 garlic cloves, squashed
½ red chilli, roughly chopped
bunch of basil, roughly torn
sea salt
1 ball mozzarella, roughly chopped
20g/¾oz/scant ¼ cup grated Parmesan cheese

Make the pizza dough according to the recipe on p.80. Lightly flour a large flat baking tray.

Divide the dough into 2 equal pieces and knead each for 2 minutes. Place on the prepared baking tray, cover with a cloth and leave to rise for 1 hour, or until doubled in size.

Preheat the oven to 220°C (fan)/240°C/475°F/Gas mark 9.

For the topping, mix together the tomatoes, extra virgin olive oil, garlic, chilli, basil and some salt in a roasting tin and bake in the oven for about 15 minutes, or until the tomatoes have softened.

Top the pizza bases with the tomato sauce followed by the mozzarella and grated Parmesan. Bake in the oven for about 10 minutes.

Remove from the oven, drizzle with a little extra virgin olive oil and serve immediately.

Although not entirely gluten-free, this Alpine-inspired pizza uses the healthier alternative flours of spelt and buckwheat to make the base. The simple topping of red onion goes really well with strong, nutty-flavoured Gruyère cheese and speck, a smoked salt-cured ham from the northern Alpine regions. Try it for a different pizza.

PIZZA DI GRANO SARACENO
Spelt and Buckwheat Pizza with Speck and Gruyère

Makes 1 round pizza, about 30cm/12in in diameter

FOR THE DOUGH:
7g/¼oz fresh yeast
175ml/6fl oz/¾ cup lukewarm water
200g/7oz/scant 1⅔ cups wholemeal (wholewheat) spelt flour
50g/1¾oz/scant ½ cup buckwheat flour
3g salt
FOR THE TOPPING:
2 tbsp extra virgin olive oil
1 large red onion, sliced
3 thyme sprigs
60g/2¼oz/½ cup Gruyère cheese, grated
4 slices of speck

Dissolve the yeast in the lukewarm water.

Mix the flours and salt together on a clean work surface. Add the yeast mixture and mix into a dough. Knead the dough for 10 minutes, then form into a ball, wrap in clingfilm and leave to rest in a warm place for 1 hour, or until doubled in size.

Preheat the oven to 200°C (fan)/220°C/425°F/Gas mark 7. Lightly grease a flat baking tray with a little extra virgin olive oil.

For the topping, heat the extra virgin olive oil in a frying pan over a medium heat, add the thyme and allow to infuse for 1 minute. Add the onion and stir-fry for a minute, then reduce the heat, cover with a lid and cook until softened. Remove from the heat and set aside.

Form the risen dough into a round pizza base and place on the prepared baking tray. Top with the cooked onions and Gruyère, and bake in the oven for 10 minutes. Remove from the oven, arrange slices of speck on top and serve.

This traditional dish from Abruzzo originated as a poor man's food using up leftovers to make a nourishing meal. As with all poor dishes, this is now a recognised local speciality at home and in restaurants, making a healthy, gluten-free alternative to classic pizza. The base is made with a simple polenta, which is then slow-baked in the oven. The topping is made with local greens and I have opted for long-stem broccoli, easily available and tasty. The addition of dried and roasted peppers, available from good delis, adds a lovely, slightly smoky aroma to this delicious rustic dish.

PIZZA E FOJE
Polenta Pizza with Greens

Makes 2 round pizzas,
about 20cm/8in
in diameter

FOR THE BASE:
extra virgin olive oil,
for drizzling
about 1.2 litres/2 pints/
5 cups water
1 tsp salt
300g/10½oz/scant 2½
cups quick-cook polenta
(cornmeal)
40g/1½oz/⅓ cup grated
Parmesan cheese
FOR THE TOPPING:
400g/14oz long-stem
broccoli
3 tbsp extra virgin olive oil
2 garlic cloves, whole
and crushed
2 dried red peppers,
deseeded and roughly
chopped in chunks
1 roasted red pepper,
drained if preserved in oil,
chopped into strips
salt

Preheat the oven to 180°C (fan)/200°C/400°F/Gas mark 6. Grease 2 round shallow terracotta dishes or 20cm/8in sandwich cake tins with a little extra virgin olive oil.

Place the water and salt in a non-stick saucepan, bring to the boil, then gradually add the polenta, stirring all the time with a wooden spoon or whisk until well amalgamated. Reduce the heat and, still stirring, cook according to the packet instructions. Quick polenta usually takes about 5 minutes. Remove from the heat and stir in the grated Parmesan. Pour the polenta into the prepared dishes or tins, level out and drizzle with a little extra virgin olive oil. Bake in the oven for about 50 minutes until slightly golden.

Meanwhile, make the topping. Cook the broccoli in a pan of boiling water for 5 minutes, then drain. Heat the extra virgin olive oil in a frying pan over a medium heat, add the garlic and peppers, and stir-fry for 2 minutes. Remove the peppers and set aside. Add the broccoli and a little salt to taste and stir-fry for about 5 minutes to allow the flavours to infuse. It's fine if the broccoli is a little overdone. Remove from the heat and discard the garlic.

Top the bases with the broccoli and dried and roasted peppers. Serve immediately.

Mini *pizzette* are so common in Italian bakeries and takeaways to have as food on the go. This traditional topping of Pizza Margherita is always a winner.

PIZZETTE MARGHERITA
Mini Pizzas with Tomato, Mozzarella and Basil

Makes 5 *pizzette*

½ quantity of Basic Pizza Dough (see p.80)
FOR THE TOPPING:
6 tbsp tomato passata (strained tomatoes)
extra virgin olive oil, for drizzling
salt
1 ball mozzarella, drained and roughly chopped
a few basil leaves

Make the pizza dough according to the recipe on p.80. Lightly flour several large flat baking trays.

Divide the dough into 5 equal pieces, about 80g/3oz each and knead each one for 2 minutes. Form into balls, cover with a cloth, and leave to rest in a warm place for 1 hour, or until doubled in size.

Preheat the oven to 220°C (fan)/240°C/475°F/Gas mark 9.

Combine the tomato passata with a drizzle of extra virgin olive oil and some salt to taste.

Roll out the balls of dough into small rounds, about 10cm/4in in diameter and place on the prepared baking trays. Spread a little tomato mixture onto each *pizzetta*, top with the mozzarella, a couple of basil leaves and a drizzle of extra virgin olive oil. Bake in the oven for about 10 minutes.

PIZZETTE DI FUNGHI
Mini Pizzas with Mushrooms

Makes 5 *pizzette*

½ quantity of Basic Pizza Dough (see p.80)
FOR THE TOPPING:
4 tbsp extra virgin olive oil
80g/3oz pancetta, finely sliced
1 garlic clove, finely sliced
½ red chilli, finely chopped
needles of 1 rosemary branch
320g/1½oz mushrooms of your choice, finely sliced

Make the pizza dough according to the recipe on p.80. Lightly flour several large flat baking trays.

Divide the dough into 5 equal pieces, about 80g/3oz each and knead each one for 2 minutes. Form into balls, cover with a cloth and leave to rest in a warm place for 1 hour.

Preheat the oven to 220°C (fan)/240°C/475°F/Gas mark 9.

For the topping, heat the extra virgin olive oil in a pan over a medium heat, add the pancetta, garlic, chilli and rosemary, and stir-fry for 2 minutes taking care not to burn the garlic. Add the mushrooms and continue to fry for a further 3 minutes until the mushrooms are cooked. Remove from the heat and set aside.

Roll each ball of dough into small rounds, about 10cm/4in in diameter and place on the prepared baking trays. Top each *pizzetta* with the mushroom mixture and bake in the oven for about 10 minutes.

Parma ham and rocket go really well together and this is a popular pizza topping. Remember the rocket is put on after the pizza is cooked for a fresh flavour.

PIZZETTE CON PROSCIUTTO E RUCOLA
Mini Pizzas with Parma Ham and Rocket

Makes 5 *pizzette*

½ quantity of Basic Pizza Dough (see p.80)
FOR THE TOPPING:
extra virgin olive oil
5 slices Parma ham (prosciutto)
1 ball of mozzarella, drained and roughly chopped
large handful of rocket (arugula)

Make the pizza dough according to the recipe on p.80. Lightly flour several large flat baking trays.

Divide the dough into 5 equal pieces, about 80g/3oz each and knead each one for 2 minutes. Form into balls, cover with a cloth and leave to rest in a warm place for 1 hour, or until doubled in size.

Preheat the oven to 220°C (fan)/240°C/475°F/Gas mark 9.

Roll out the balls of dough into small rounds, about 10cm/4in in diameter and place on the prepared baking trays. Spread a little extra virgin olive oil over each one and top with a slice of Parma ham and some mozzarella. Bake in the oven for about 10 minutes.

Remove from the oven and top with some rocket and a drizzle of extra virgin olive oil.

Scapece is a southern Italian way of cooking courgettes giving them an extra kick with an infusion of mint and vinegar, then lightly deep-frying before serving them as a salad. It also makes a lovely, different pizza topping.

PIZZETTE ALLA SCAPECE
Mini Pizzas Topped with Courgettes and Mint

Makes 5 *pizzette*

½ quantity of Basic Pizza Dough (see p.80)
FOR THE TOPPING:
360g/12oz courgette (zucchini), finely sliced
vegetable oil, for deep-frying
2 tsp chopped mint leaves
1 garlic clove, finely chopped
1 tbsp white wine vinegar
1 tbsp extra virgin olive oil
salt

Make the pizza dough according to the recipe on p.80. Lightly flour several large flat baking trays.

Divide the dough into 5 equal pieces, about 80g/3oz each and knead each one for 2 minutes. Form into balls, cover with a cloth, and leave to rest in a warm place for 1 hour, or until doubled in size.

Heat some vegetable oil in a deep pan over a medium-high heat, add the courgettes and deep-fry until golden brown on both sides. Drain on kitchen paper. Mix the mint, garlic, vinegar, extra virgin olive oil and a little salt together, then pour over the courgettes and leave to infuse for 30 minutes.

Preheat the oven to 220°C (fan)/240°C/475°F/Gas mark 9.

Form each piece of dough into small rounds, about 10cm/4in in diameter and top with the courgettes. Bake in the oven for about 10 minutes.

Saltinbocca is another variation of the 'Pizza Family'. The dough puffs up in the oven during baking, becoming an oval balloon of hot air! It is then slit and filled, returning to the oven for a couple of minutes. This typical Neapolitan filling goes really well with this pitta-type bread. The secret is to get the dough as thin as you possibly can.

SALTINBOCCA ALLA SORRENTINA
Saltinbocca with Aubergines

Makes 6

10g/¼oz fresh yeast
325ml/11fl oz/scant 1½ cups lukewarm water
500g/1lb 2oz/4 cups strong white bread flour
2 tsp salt
FOR THE FILLING:
3 tbsp extra virgin olive oil
1 garlic clove, whole and crushed
600g/1lb 5oz aubergine (eggplant),
    cut into small cubes
10 cherry tomatoes, deseeded and roughly chopped
handful of basil leaves, torn
pinch of salt
1 ball of smoked mozzarella, drained and cut into
    small pieces
20g/¾oz/scant ¼ cup grated pecorino cheese

Dissolve the yeast in the lukewarm water.

Mix the flour and salt together in a large bowl, add the yeast mixture and mix into a dough. Knead the dough for about 10 minutes until it is smooth and elastic. Form into a ball, cover with clingfilm and leave to rest in a warm place for 1 hour, or until doubled in size.

Meanwhile, make the filling. Heat the extra virgin olive oil in a frying pan over a medium heat, add the garlic and sauté for a minute. Add the aubergine cubes and stir-fry for about 10 minutes until golden and cooked. Stir in the cherry tomatoes and cook for a further 2 minutes. Add the basil leaves and some salt to taste, then remove from the heat, discard the garlic and set aside.

Preheat the oven to 220°C (fan)/240°C/475°F/Gas mark 9 and line a flat baking tray with parchment paper.

Divide the dough into 6 equal pieces. Flatten each piece as much as you can by stretching with your hands into a roughly rectangular shape. Place on the prepared tray and bake in the oven for about 10 minutes, or until well risen and golden brown.

Remove from the oven and, using a sharp serrated knife, open the *saltimbocca*. Spread the inside with the aubergine filling, mozzarella, grated pecorino and a drizzle of extra virgin olive oil, then return to the oven for 2 minutes until the mozzarella has melted.

Remove from the oven, close the *saltimbocca*, flatten slightly and serve.

Calzone, literally translated as 'trouser', is basically a pizza which is folded over and is typical of Neapolitan street food. It probably originated for ease of eating while out and about. You can fill it with almost anything you like, rather like pizza toppings. *Calzone* can be made smaller and sometimes known as *panzerotti*, and can be fried instead of baked. In Sicily, *calzone* is known as *cuddurini*.

CALZONE
Basic *Calzone*

Makes 6 *calzone*

10g/¼oz fresh yeast
325ml/11oz/scant 1½ cups lukewarm water
500g/1lb 2oz/4 cups strong white bread flour
2 tsp salt

Dissolve the yeast in the lukewarm water.

Mix the flour and salt together on a clean work surface. Add the yeast mixture and mix into a dough. Knead the dough for 10 minutes until smooth and elastic, then form into a ball, cover with clingfilm and leave to rest in a warm place for 1 hour, or until doubled in size.

Preheat the oven to 220°C (fan)/240°C/475°F/Gas mark 9 and line a flat baking tray with parchment paper.

Knock back the dough and divide into 6 equal pieces. Roll each piece into a ball on a lightly floured work surface and flatten and stretch with your hands. With the help of a rolling pin, roll each dough ball out into a circular shape. Place a little of your chosen filling in the middle of each dough circle, keeping a border of 3cm/1¼in all round. Brush the border with water and fold one half over, pressing down well to make a crescent shape. Place on the prepared baking tray, brush with a little extra virgin olive oil and bake in the oven for 12 minutes.

FILLINGS:
Tomato, ham and mozarella (see p.110)
Escarole and pitted black olives (see p.111)
Cherry tomatoes, mozzarella and grated Parmesan cheese
Sliced ham and grated Parmesan cheese
Ricotta and sliced red onion

This basic filling for *calzone* is probably the best known and loved, not only in Italy but all over the world.

CALZONE RIPIENO DI POMODORO, PROSCIUTTO E MOZZARELLA
Calzone Filled with Tomato, Ham and Mozzarella

Makes 6 *calzone*

10g/¼oz fresh yeast
325ml/11fl oz/scant 1½ cups lukewarm water
500g/1lb 2oz/4 cups plain (all-purpose) flour
2 tsp salt
FOR THE FILLING:
200ml/7fl oz tomato passata (strained tomatoes)
1 tbsp extra virgin olive oil
pinch of salt
1 ball of mozzarella, drained and chopped into small
    pieces
6 small slices of cooked ham

Dissolve the yeast in the lukewarm water.

Mix the flour and salt together in a large bowl. Add the yeast mixture and mix into a dough. Knead the dough for 10 minutes until smooth and elastic, then form a ball, cover with clingfilm, and leave to rest in a warm place for 1 hour, or until doubled in size.

Meanwhile, make the filling. Place the passata in a small bowl and mix with the extra virgin olive oil and salt.

Preheat the oven to 220°C (fan)/240°C/475°F/Gas mark 9 and line a flat baking tray with parchment paper.

Knock back the dough and divide into 6 equal pieces. Roll each piece into a ball and flatten and stretch with your hands. With the help of a rolling pin, roll each dough ball out into a circular shape. Spread a little of the tomato sauce in the middle of each circle, keeping a border of 3cm/1¼in all round. Top with a slice of ham and pieces of mozzarella, then brush the border with water and fold one half over, pressing down well to make a crescent shape. Place on the prepared tray, brush with a little extra virgin olive oil and bake for 12 minutes.

This typical southern Italian vegetable is one of my favourites and very popular used to fill *calzone* or even to top pizza in the Neapolitan area. If you can't find escarole then substitute it with green curly endive, which you find in the salad section in shops, or ask your greengrocer.

CALZONE RIPIENO DI SCAROLA
Calzone Filled with Escarole

Makes 6 *calzone*

FOR THE DOUGH:
1 quantity of Basic Calzone dough (see p.109)
FOR THE FILLING:
4 tbsp extra virgin olive oil, plus extra for brushing
2 garlic cloves, whole and squashed
6 anchovy fillets
12 black olives, pitted
3 bunches of escarole, cleaned, leaves separated
   and roughly chopped
salt and freshly ground black pepper

Make the calzone according to the recipe on p.109.

To make the filling, heat the extra virgin olive oil in a pan over a medium heat, add the garlic and sauté for a minute or so until golden. Discard the garlic, add the anchovies and olives and sauté for another minute until the anchovies dissolve. Stir in the escarole, then cover with a lid and cook over a low-medium heat for about 8–10 minutes until wilted and cooked. Check for seasoning, adding salt and pepper if necessary, then remove from the heat and leave to cool.

Preheat the oven to 220°C (fan)/240°C/475°F/Gas mark 9 and line a flat baking tray with parchment paper.

Knock back the dough and divide into 6 equal pieces. Roll each piece into a ball and flatten and stretch with your hands. With the help of a rolling pin, roll each dough ball out into a circular shape. Place a little of the filling in the middle of each circle, keeping a border of 3cm/1¼in all round. Brush the border with water and fold one half over, pressing down well to make a crescent shape. Place the *calzone* on the prepared baking tray, brush with a little extra virgin olive oil and bake in the oven for 12 minutes.

A ricotta filling is very common in *calzone* especially with red onion. To give it a twist, I have added pieces of salami, which gives a kick to the ricotta.

CALZONE CON RICOTTA E SALAME
Calzone with Ricotta and Salami

Makes 6 *calzone*

FOR THE DOUGH:
1 quantity of Basic Calzone dough (see p.109)
extra virgin olive oil, for drizzling
FOR THE FILLING:
250g/9oz/generous 1 cup ricotta, drained
1 ball of mozzarella, drained and roughly chopped in
   small cubes
50g/1¾oz salami, cut into small pieces
25g/1oz/scant ¼ cup grated Parmesan cheese
salt and freshly ground black pepper
2 tsp finely chopped parsley

Make the *calzone* according to the recipe on p.109.

To make the filling, combine all the ingredients together and set aside.

Preheat the oven to 220°C (fan)/240°C/475°F/Gas mark 9 and line a flat baking tray with parchment paper.

Knock back the dough and divide into 6 equal pieces. Roll each piece into a ball and flatten and stretch with your hands. With the help of a rolling pin, roll each dough ball out into a circular shape. Place a little of the filling in the middle of each circle, keeping a border of 3cm/1¼in all round. Brush the border with water and fold one half over, pressing down well to make a crescent shape. Place the *calzone* on the prepared baking tray, brush with a little extra virgin olive oil and bake in the oven for 12 minutes.

This is another popular *calzone* filling as well as pizza topping in southern Italy, where the broccoli used is known as *cime di rape*, which in England are raab tops and not easily available. I have therefore substituted this vegetable with long-stem broccoli.

CALZONE CON SALSICCIA E BROCCOLI
Calzone with Sausage and Broccoli

Makes 6 *calzone*

FOR THE DOUGH:
1 quantity of Basic Calzone dough (see p.109)
FOR THE FILLING:
500g/1lb 2oz long-stem broccoli, trimmed
3 tbsp extra virgin olive oil
1 garlic clove, whole and squashed
3 good-quality pork sausages, skin removed
   and crumbled
salt

Make the calzone according to the recipe on p.109.

To make the filling, blanch the broccoli for 2 minutes, then drain and set aside. Heat the extra virgin olive oil in a pan over a medium heat, add the garlic and sweat for 2 minutes, then discard. Add the crumbled sausages and broccoli, a little salt to taste and stir-fry over a medium heat for 1 minute. Reduce the heat, cover with a lid and cook for about 10–15 minutes until the sausage is cooked through and the broccoli is tender but not mushy.

Preheat the oven to 220°C (fan)/240°C/475°F/Gas mark 9 and line a flat baking tray with parchment paper.

Knock back the dough and divide into 6 equal pieces. Roll each piece into a ball and flatten and stretch with your hands. With the help of a rolling pin, roll each dough ball out into a circular shape. Place a little of the filling in the middle of each dough circle, keeping a border of 3cm/1¼in all round. Brush the border with water and fold one half over, pressing down well to make a crescent shape. Place the *calzone* on the prepared baking tray, brush with a little extra virgin olive oil and bake in the oven for 12 minutes.

TORTE SALATE   Savoury Pies and Tarts

When thinking of savoury pies and tarts, one immediately thinks of England and its meat pies or France and its quiches. However, Italy has a variety of its own versions known as *torte salate*, literally translated as 'savoury cakes'.

Torte salate apparently have age-old roots dating back to pagan times and when agriculture played an important part of life. To celebrate and give thanks for the first seasonal vegetables, a type of pie would often be made. This was usually at Easter time when all the lovely spring greens would come alive in the orchards and gardens, hence classic dishes such as *Torta Pasqualina*, *Erbazzone* and *Torta Verde* came to being and are still very much part of Italian cooking.

Torte salate were a good way of making bread dough go further, adding fillings of whatever bits of leftovers were available to make a substantial meal for the family. I remember on bread-making day in our house, we would often have a dish like this to enjoy either as part of a meal or to have as a snack. *Torte salate* are common to take on picnics as they contain all the goodness and nourishment you need. They are also popular to serve as a starter with perhaps some other antipasto dishes, usually for special occasions – a large *torta salata* is placed the middle of the table and everyone will have a small slice. These days I enjoy a slice or two of a *torta salata* for lunch or dinner with a side salad.

Torte salate are also made with pastry; the traditional pastry, sometimes known as *pasta matta*, is a simple mix of flour, salt, extra virgin olive oil and water, and this is still used today for many tarts like the popular *Erbazzone* (see p.116). It is quick and simple to make, with no need to rest in the refrigerator, and easy to roll out. The lack of butter also makes it a healthier option and its bland taste makes it perfect to combine with all sorts of savoury fillings.

Pastries for savoury pies have evolved in Italy and rich shortcrust pastries, known as *pasta frolla*, are also used for tarts and pies.

This savoury pie, also known as *Scarpazzone*, is a rustic dish from Emilia Romagna. Its humble origins used whatever seasonal greens were available, usually from the garden, and perhaps some local cheese to add flavour. It was traditionally cooked in a round copper dish, known in local dialect as *al sol*, in the wood-fired oven where bread was baked. It is still a popular dish in the region and still cooked with local greens. In my version, I have used Swiss chard including the white stems, which I always leave in dishes to add more flavour. You could substitute with spinach. And if you want to make it vegetarian, just omit the prosciutto.

ERBAZZONE
Green Vegetable Pie

Serves 8

FOR THE PASTRY:
400g/14oz/scant 3¼ cups plain (all-purpose) flour, sifted
8g/scant ¼oz/1¼ tsp salt
30ml/1fl oz/2 tbsp extra virgin olive oil
200ml/7fl oz/scant 1 cup water
FOR THE FILLING:
40ml/1½fl oz/3 tbsp extra virgin olive oil, plus extra for brushing
2 garlic cloves, finely chopped
100g/3½oz prosciutto, finely sliced
150g/5½oz leeks, finely chopped
1kg/2lb 4oz Swiss chard, roughly chopped
salt and freshly ground black pepper
150g/5½oz/1⅓ cups grated Parmesan cheese

To make the pastry, combine the flour and salt in a large bowl, add the extra virgin olive oil and water, and work into a smooth dough. Wrap in clingfilm and leave to chill while you make the filling.

Heat the extra virgin olive oil in a large pan over a medium heat, add the garlic and prosciutto, and stir-fry until the prosciutto crisps up. Add the leeks and sweat for 2 minutes. Add the Swiss chard, salt and pepper to taste, and cook over a medium-low heat for about 15 minutes, or until tender. Remove from the heat, leave to cool, drain off any excess liquid and stir in 100g/3½oz/1 cup grated Parmesan.

Preheat the oven to 160°C (fan)/180°C/350°F/Gas mark 4 and lightly grease a 28cm/11in round loose-bottomed tart tin with extra virgin olive oil.

Divide the pastry in half, one slightly bigger, about 380g/13¼oz. Roll out the bigger piece on a lightly floured work surface and use to line the prepared tin. Fill the pastry case with the chard filling and sprinkle with the remaining grated Parmesan. Roll out the other piece of pastry, then place over the top and seal the edges. Prick all over with a fork, brush with a little extra virgin olive oil and bake in the oven for 30–35 minutes until golden. Leave to cool slightly and eat warm.

A delicious rustic savoury pie made with bread dough and filled with my favourite southern Italian vegetable. It is delicious enjoyed hot or cold. When I was a young boy, we would take a nutritious pie like this with us on picnics or days out and you didn't really need anything else.

TORTA SALATA CON SCAROLA
Savoury Pie with Escarole

Serves 4–6

FOR THE DOUGH:
10g/¼oz fresh yeast
150ml/5fl oz/⅔ cup
  lukewarm water
250g/9oz/2 cups strong
  white bread flour
pinch of salt
20ml/¾fl oz/4 tsp olive oil
FOR THE FILLING:
4 tbsp extra virgin olive oil
2 garlic cloves, left whole
4 anchovy fillets
800g/1lb 12oz escarole,
  sliced into small strips
25g/1oz/scant ¼ cup
  capers
50g/1¾oz/generous ¼ cup
  pitted black olives
25g/1oz/scant ¼ cup pine
  kernels
salt and freshly ground
  black pepper
75g/2¾oz provolone (or
  mature Cheddar) cheese,
  cut into small cubes

Dissolve the yeast in the lukewarm water. Combine the flour and salt in a large bowl, add the yeast mixture and olive oil and mix into a dough. Knead for about 10 minutes until smooth and elastic. Cover with clingfilm and leave to rest in a warm place for 1 hour, or until doubled in size.

Meanwhile, make the filling. Heat the extra virgin olive oil in a large frying pan over a medium heat, add the garlic and anchovies, and sweat until the anchovies have dissolved and the garlic is golden. Remove the garlic and discard. Add the escarole and stir-fry for 1 minute. Add the capers, olives and pine kernels and some salt and pepper to taste and mix well. Reduce the heat to low, cover with a lid and cook for about 15 minutes until the escarole is tender. Remove from the heat and stir in the provolone.

Meanwhile, preheat the oven to 200°C (fan)/220°C/425°F/ Gas mark 7 and line a 23cm/9in round pie dish with parchment paper.

Divide the dough in half, one piece a little bigger than the other. Roll out the larger piece on a lightly floured work surface to a roughly round shape and use to line the pie dish. Fill with the escarole mixture. Roll out the remaining dough and place over the top of the filling, pressing down to seal the edges. Prick all over with a fork and bake in the oven for 30–35 minutes until golden all over.

Remove from the oven, rest for 10 minutes, then serve.

Instead of the usual bread dough, I have made a shortcrust pastry for this pie with a little lard, adding richness. If you prefer, you can omit the lard and add extra butter. The *guanciale* (pork cheek) really makes this dish – you could substitute with pancetta, but I urge you to get *guanciale* – a good Italian deli will stock it. The pie is simple to make – if you are in a rush, you can buy the pastry ready-made. The excess pastry that lines the pie is folded over and pinched, leaving most of the filling exposed, which looks pretty when served. You can also enjoy this pie cold – in fact, I prefer it the day after when all the flavours have infused nicely. It is quite filling, so I would serve it with perhaps just a side salad. *Illustrated on p.118.*

TORTA SALATA APERTA CON SPINACI, E GUANCIALE E POMODORINI SECCHI

Open Savoury Pie with Spinach, *Guanciale* and Sun-Dried Tomatoes

Serves 4–6

FOR THE PASTRY:
340g/12oz/2¾ cups plain (all-purpose) flour
pinch of salt
110g/4oz/½ cup cold unsalted butter, diced
50g/1¾oz/scant ¼ cup cold lard, diced
about 6 tbsp ice-cold water
FOR THE FILLING:
1 tbsp extra virgin olive oil
1 small onion, finely diced
200g/7oz *guanciale*, cubed
4 sun-dried tomatoes, roughly chopped
60g/2¼oz/⅓ cup green pitted olives, sliced or left whole, depending on size
1 tbsp tomato concentrate mixed with a splash of white wine
freshly ground black pepper
500g/1lb 2oz spinach
2 eggs, beaten
20g/¾oz/scant ¼ cup grated Parmesan cheese
2 cherry tomatoes, halved
1 egg yolk, beaten

For the pastry, combine the flour and salt in a large bowl, add the butter and lard and rub them into the flour until it resembles breadcrumbs. Add enough ice-cold water to make a smooth dough, wrap in clingfilm and leave to chill for at least 30 minutes.

Preheat the oven to 190°C (fan)/200°C/400°F/Gas mark 6 and line a 24cm/9½in round ceramic or terracotta flan dish with parchment paper.

Heat the oil in a large pan over a medium heat, add the onion and *guanciale* and sweat until the onion has softened. Stir in the sun-dried tomatoes, olives and tomato concentrate and season with a little black pepper. Add the spinach and cook for a minute or so until the spinach has wilted. Remove from the heat and leave to cool. Remove excess oil if necessary. Stir in the beaten eggs and Parmesan and set aside.

Roll out the pastry on a lightly floured work surface to a circular shape of about 1cm/½in thick and use to line the flan tin. Make sure you have excess pastry all around the edges. Pour the filling inside the pastry case and fold over the excess pastry, pinching at regular intervals. Most of the filling will be visible. Arrange the sliced tomatoes on top and bake in the oven for 50 minutes. About halfway through the cooking time, brush the pastry with egg yolk and continue to bake until cooked and golden.

Remove from the oven, leave to rest for 5 minutes, then slice and serve. This can also be enjoyed eaten cold.

This delicious pie is made with a pastry known as *pasta matta* which translates as 'crazy pastry'! I don't know why it has this bizarre name, but it is a pastry often made in Italy for both sweet and savoury delicacies. Quick and simple to make, it is easy to roll out as it does not tend to crack, and is much lighter due to the low fat content. The filling of ricotta and courgettes combines really well and the addition of grilled courgettes in a lattice pattern makes this a very pretty pie indeed, as well as being delicious to eat! Perfect served with a mixed salad for a light lunch or it can be enjoyed cold on a picnic. *Illustrated on p.119.*

TORTA RUSTICA CON ZUCCHINE E RICOTTA
Courgette and Ricotta Pie

Serves 6

FOR THE PASTRY:
400g/14oz/scant 3¼ cups plain (all-purpose) flour, sifted
pinch of salt
6 tbsp extra virgin olive oil
150ml/5fl oz/⅔ cup fizzy mineral water
FOR THE FILLING:
3 large courgettes (zucchini)
1 tbsp extra virgin olive oil
40g/1½oz pancetta, cut into small cubes
1 small onion, finely chopped
250g/9oz/generous 1 cup ricotta
1 egg
handful of basil leaves, roughly torn
40g/1½oz/⅓ cup grated Parmesan cheese
salt and freshly ground black pepper
egg wash (see p.13)

To make the pastry, combine the flour and salt in a large bowl or work surface, make a well in the centre, add the extra virgin olive oil and gradually add the mineral water to form a soft dough. Form into a ball, wrap in clingfilm and leave to rest at room temperature for about 20 minutes.

Cut 2 courgettes lengthways into 5mm/¼in thick slices. Heat a griddle over a high heat and grill the courgettes on each side until they soften, then remove and set aside.

Preheat the oven to 170°C (fan)/190°C/375°F/Gas mark 5. Line a 24cm/9½in round pie dish with parchment paper, and finely slice the remaining courgette.

Heat the extra virgin olive oil in a pan, add the pancetta and onion and stir-fry over a medium heat until the pancetta is nearly crispy and the onion has softened. Add the sliced courgette, reduce the heat to low, cover with a lid and cook for about 5 minutes until the courgette has softened. Remove from the heat, drain any liquid and leave to cool.

Combine the ricotta, egg, basil, Parmesan, black pepper and courgette mixture in a bowl. Season with salt to taste.

Roll out the pastry on a lightly floured work surface to about 2mm/⅙in thick and use to line a pie dish, making sure you have some excess pastry around the edges. Fill with the filling mixture. Place the courgette strips in a lattice pattern over the filling, then fold over the excess pastry, pinching it at regular intervals. Brush the pastry and courgettes with egg wash and bake for about 25 minutes until golden.

Remove from the oven, rest for 5 minutes, slice and serve.

Savoury pies like this one were often made when I was a child in Italy, especially on bread-making days when we had leftover dough and whatever produce was around would be used as a filling. This pie is ideal to make during spring when fresh broad beans are available, however, it is just as good with frozen ones. If you are using fresh, remember to remove the skin after podding. The addition of preserved artichokes really gives a kick to this dish, and with the added potatoes, this is a substantial meal in itself.

TORTA SALATA CON FAVE E CARCIOFI
Savoury Pie with Broad Beans and Artichokes

Serves 4–6

FOR THE DOUGH:
10g/¼oz fresh yeast
150ml/5fl oz/⅔ cup
    lukewarm water
250g/9oz/2 cups strong
    white bread flour
pinch of salt
25g/1oz/2 tbsp unsalted
    butter, room temperature,
    cut into pieces
FOR THE FILLING:
300g/10½oz potatoes,
    peeled and sliced into
    1cm/½in rounds
salt and freshly ground
    black pepper
2 tbsp extra virgin olive oil,
    plus extra for drizzling
1 banana shallot,
    finely chopped
150g/5½oz broad (fava)
    beans, shelled
1 x 285g/10oz jar of
    preserved artichokes
    (discard the oil)
70g/2½oz Parma ham
    (prosciutto), chopped
3 egg yolks, beaten
3 tbsp milk
40g/1½oz/⅓ cup grated
    Parmesan cheese
1 egg yolk, beaten

Dissolve the yeast in the lukewarm water. Combine the flour, salt and butter in a large bowl. Make a well in the centre, gradually pour in the yeast mixture and mix well to form a soft dough. Knead on the work surface for 10 minutes, then form into a ball, cover with a cloth and leave to rise in a warm place for 1 hour, or until doubled in size.

Preheat the oven to 200°C (fan)/220°C/425°F/Gas mark 7 and line a 23cm/9in round pie dish with parchment paper. Lightly grease a baking tray.

Place the potato rounds on the prepared baking tray, sprinkle with some salt and pepper, and drizzle with some extra virgin olive oil. Roast in the oven for about 10 minutes until golden and cooked through. Remove from the oven and set aside.

Heat the oil in a frying pan over a medium heat, add the shallots and broad beans and sauté until the broad beans are soft. Remove from the heat and leave to cool. Once cool, combine with the artichokes, ham, egg yolks, milk, Parmesan and some salt and pepper to taste. Set aside.

Divide the dough in half. Roll out one piece on a lightly floured work surface and use to line the pie dish. Fill the pie with the vegetable filling, then roll out the other piece of dough and use to cover the pie, sealing well so that the filling does not escape. Prick all over with a fork and bake in the oven for about 35 minutes until golden. About halfway through the cooking time, brush the top of the pie with some beaten egg yolk.

Remove from the oven, leave to rest for 5 minutes and serve. This is delicious served hot or cold.

This tasty, rustic mushroom pie is made with a variety of flours, making the dough light and full of flavour. The filling is simply made with cultivated white mushrooms, but you could substitute with the wild variety in season if you prefer. It is tied like a *fagotto* or a knapsack which makes it look really pretty when presented at the table. It is delicious eaten hot or cold with a salad.

FAGOTTO DI FUNGHI CON FARINE MISTE
Mixed Grains Mushroom Pie

Serves 4–6

FOR THE BREAD DOUGH:
12g fresh yeast
150ml/5fl oz/⅔ cup
    lukewarm water
250g/9oz/2 cups plain (all-
    purpose) flour
25g/1oz/scant ¼ cup
    buckwheat flour
25g/1oz/scant ¼ cup
    polenta (cornmeal)
25g/1oz/scant ¼ cup
    Italian chickpea flour
1 tsp salt
1 egg
FOR THE FILLING:
50ml/1¾fl oz/scant ¼ cup
    extra virgin olive oil
60g/2¼oz pancetta, diced
1 leek, finely sliced
3 thyme sprigs, leaves only
600g/1lb 5oz mushrooms
    of your choice, sliced
salt and freshly ground
    black pepper
splash of white wine
egg wash (see p.13)

Dissolve the yeast in the lukewarm water. Combine the flours and salt in a large bowl, add the yeast mixture and egg and mix well into a dough. Knead for 10 minutes, cover with clingfilm and leave to rest in a warm place for about 1 hour, or until doubled in size.

To make the filling, heat the extra virgin olive oil in a pan over a high heat, add the pancetta, leek and thyme, and stir-fry for 3–4 minutes. Stir in the mushrooms, then add some salt and pepper. Add the wine and allow to evaporate, about 1 minute. Reduce the heat to medium, cover with a lid and cook for 5 minutes.

Preheat the oven to 160°C (fan)/180°C/350°F/Gas mark 4. Line a pie dish or a flat baking tray with parchment paper.

Roll out the dough into a thin square sheet big enough to line the pie dish or baking tray and place in the prepared pie dish or baking tray. Prick the dough all over with a fork. Place the mushroom filling in the centre, then take the 4 corners of the dough and make into a parcel (see photo). Tie with kitchen string and brush all over with egg wash. Bake in the oven for 45 minutes.

Remove from the oven, leave to rest for 5 minutes, then slice and serve.

This lovely savoury tart is the exact opposite of the sweet version so loved in Naples at Easter time (see p.175). If you looked at it not knowing it was savoury, you could easily mistake it for the classic sweet one. Deliciously tasty and rich, it is made with a variety of cheeses and cured meats – a great way of using up leftovers! Use whatever you have, you don't have to use the same as in this recipe. Although it is delicious hot, it is best sliced and served when left to rest for a while.

PASTIERA SALATA
Savoury Neapolitan Wheat Tart

Serves 8

FOR THE PASTRY:
450g/15oz/scant 3⅔ cups plain (all-purpose) flour, sifted
pinch of salt
40g/1½oz/⅓ cup grated Parmesan cheese
120ml/4fl oz/½ cup olive oil
3 egg yolks
about 4 tbsp cold water

FOR THE FILLING:
300g/10½oz pre-cooked wheat (sold in jars from good Italian delis or online)
200ml/7fl oz/scant 1 cup milk
40g/1½oz/3 tbsp unsalted butter
300g/10½oz/1¼ cups ricotta
4 egg yolks
80g/3oz provolone (or mature Cheddar) cheese, cut into small cubes
80g/3oz fontina cheese, cut into small cubes
80g/3oz/¾ cup grated Parmesan cheese
20g/¾oz/¼ cup grated pecorino cheese
100g/3½oz Neapolitan salami, cut into small cubes
60g/2¼oz mortadella, roughly chopped

To make the pastry, combine the flour, salt and Parmesan in a large bowl. Mix in the olive oil and egg yolks and gradually add enough cold water to form a smooth pastry. Wrap in clingfilm and leave to rest at room temperature while you make the filling.

Place the wheat, milk and butter in a saucepan and cook over a medium heat, stirring with a wooden spoon, until the milk is absorbed and it is a creamy consistency. Remove from the heat and allow to cool.

Preheat the oven to 160°C (fan)/180°C/350°F/Gas mark 4. Grease a 28cm/11in loose-bottomed tart tin with olive oil and dust with flour.

Mash the ricotta with a fork, mix it with the cooled wheat mixture and stir in the egg yolks, cheeses, salami, mortadella and some salt and pepper to taste. Go easy with the salt as the cheeses and cured meats will be quite salty already.

Roll out the pastry on a lightly floured work surface to a thickness of 5mm/¼in and use to line the prepared tart tin. Fill with the mixture. Reroll the remaining pieces of pastry and cut into thin strips, then place them in a criss-cross pattern over the filling.

Bake in the oven for 40–45 minutes until the cheeses have melted, the filling has puffed up nicely and is golden brown all over.

Remove from the oven and rest for at least 20 minutes before serving.

I don't normally encourage people to buy pastry, but puff pastry is quite a tricky one to master and get right. So for this recipe I allow myself to cheat and buy the ready-made variety which is widely available and actually very good. In Italy, it is common to fill a *torta salata* or *rotolo* with mixed bitter greens known as *erbette*, which I have never been able to find here. So I have opted for rainbow chard, which is a variety of brightly coloured Swiss chard. It is beautiful to look at, tastes delicious and works well with puff pastry. The potatoes not only add a little bulk but combine well with the chard together with delicious provolone cheese. If you can't find provolone, substitute with a good-quality mature Cheddar. Serve the *rotolo* with a tomato salad for a light meal or it can be eaten cold as a snack or for a picnic.

ROTOLO CON BIETOLE
Rainbow Chard Puff Pastry Roll

Serves 4–6

60g/2¼oz/¼ cup unsalted
   butter
1 small onion,
   finely chopped
600g/1lb 5oz rainbow
   chard, finely sliced
   (including stalks)
1 large potato, peeled and
   thinly sliced with
   a mandolin or
   cheese grater
2 tbsp grated Parmesan
   cheese
500g/1lb 2oz ready-made
   puff pastry
50g/1¾oz provolone
   cheese shavings
egg wash (see p.13)

Melt the butter in a large pan, add the onion and sauté over a medium heat until softened. Stir in the chard, season with salt and pepper, cover with a lid, reduce the heat and cook for about 10 minutes until the chard is tender but not mushy. The stalks should be 'al dente'. Stir in the potatoes and cook for a further 2 minutes. Remove from the heat and leave to cool, then stir in the Parmesan.

Preheat the oven to 170°C (fan)/190°C/375°F/Gas mark 5 and line a large flat baking tray with parchment paper.

Roll out the pastry on a lightly floured work surface into a rectangular shape about 2–3mm/¹⁄₁₆–⅛in thick. Place the filling about one-quarter of the way in from one of the longer sides of the pastry sheet, then arrange shavings of provolone on top and carefully fold over the pastry to make a roll closing both ends to form a ring. If necessary, brush some egg wash to seal. Place on the prepared baking tray. Using a small sharp knife, make incisions at about 4–5cm/1½–2in intervals and brush with egg wash. Bake in the oven for about 40 minutes until golden.

Remove from the oven, leave for 3–4 minutes, then slice over the incisions and serve. This can also be eaten cold.

This is a lovely combination of an English pie with a classic Italian chicken filling. The title *alla Cacciatora*, translated as 'in the style of the hunter', suggests it was probably first made with game birds or rabbit. As with many Italian dishes, it also has roots in the *cucina povera* where people used whatever they had to hand; in this case chicken, enriched with whatever vegetables and herbs were available to make it go further. It is made all over Italy in different ways and usually eaten with bread. It makes a wonderful filling for a pie. The pastry is a basic shortcrust, but if you prefer, you can use a sheet of ready-made puff pastry for the lid. .

TORTA SALATA CON POLLO ALLA CACCIATORA
Chicken *Cacciatora* Pie

Serves 4

FOR THE PASTRY:
250g/9oz/2 cups plain (all-
    purpose) flour, sifted
125g/4½ oz/½ cup cold
    unsalted butter, cubed
about 4 tbsp cold water
FOR THE FILLING:
4 tbsp extra virgin olive oil
1 small onion, finely chopped
½ red chilli, finely chopped
1 celery stalk, finely
    chopped
1 carrot, finely chopped
1 red (bell) pepper,
    finely chopped
450g/15oz skinless chicken
    breast, cut into chunks
salt and freshly ground
    black pepper
2 thyme sprigs
100ml/3½fl oz/scant ½ cup
    white wine
1 tbsp tomato concentrate
    with 2 tbsp warm water
175g/6oz cherry tomatoes,
    halved
250g/9oz button (white)
    mushrooms, sliced
100ml/3½ fl oz/scant ½
    cup chicken stock (broth)
1 small egg, beaten

To make the pastry, place the flour into a large bowl, add the butter and rub it in until it resembles breadcrumbs. Gradually add enough cold water to make a smooth dough. Wrap in clingfilm and leave to chill for at least 30 minutes.

To make the filling, heat the extra virgin olive oil in a large pan over a medium heat, add the onion, chilli, celery, carrot and pepper, and sauté for 5 minutes. Rub salt and pepper all over the chicken pieces, add to the pan and fry until sealed all over. Add the thyme, increase the heat, pour in the wine and allow to evaporate, about 3–4 minutes. Reduce the heat to low, stir in the tomato concentrate mixture, cherry tomatoes, mushrooms and stock, then cover with a lid and gently cook for 25 minutes. Remove from the heat and leave to cool slightly.

Meanwhile, preheat the oven to 180°C (fan)/200°C/400°F/ Gas mark 6.

When the chicken is ready, pour into a 24cm/9½in round pie dish. Roll out the pastry on a lightly floured work surface to a thickness of a pound coin and place on top of the filling, pinching the edges to seal. Brush all over with egg wash, then make an incision on the top and bake in the oven for about 30–35 minutes until golden and hot through. Serve.

These Umbrian flatbreads take their name from the stone they were traditionally cooked on known as *testo* – a flat tile which was placed on the fire to heat up and enable the circles of dough to be cooked. Quick and cheap to make, rural families made them instead of bread and often in large quantities, which were stored in a special container placed by the fireplace to be kept warm ready for when the rest of the family returned home. Nowadays the flatbreads are sliced open and filled with local cured meats and cheese. They are so popular in Umbria, particularly around Perugia, that annual *sagre* (food festivals) are held in their honour. I like to make them with oozing fontina cheese and ham and serve them as 'Italian cheese toasties' to my girls. Equally delicious filled with pesto and grated Parmesan or other fillings such as sausage, preserved vegetables, salad or whatever else you prefer.

TORTA AL TESTO
Umbrian Flatbreads

Makes 8

12g/just under ½oz fresh yeast
320ml/11¼fl oz/scant 1½ cups lukewarm water
500g/1lb 2 oz/4 cups strong white bread flour, sifted
pinch of salt
1 tbsp extra virgin olive oil
FOR THE FILLING:
fontina cheese, roughly sliced
cooked ham
basil pesto
grated Parmesan cheese

Line a large flat baking tray with parchment paper.

Dissolve the yeast in the lukewarm water.

Combine the flour and salt in a large bowl. Add the extra virgin olive oil and yeast mixture, and mix into a dough. Knead for 10 minutes, cover with clingfilm and leave to rest in a warm place for about 2 hours, or until doubled in size.

Divide the dough into 8 pieces, about 100g/3½ oz each. Roll out each piece of dough on a lightly floured work surface into about 20cm/8in rounds. Prick all over with a fork.

Heat a griddle or non-stick frying pan until very hot. Place a dough round in the pan and cook on both sides until golden brown. Repeat with the remaining dough rounds.

Preheat the oven to 180°C (fan)/200°C/400°F/Gas mark 6.

When the flatbreads are cool enough to handle, slit them open on the side, fill with ham and cheese or pesto and Parmesan, or whatever combination you prefer. Close them and place on the prepared baking tray. Bake in the oven for a few minutes until the cheese has melted and the flatbreads have warmed through. Serve immediately.

These simple, lovely polenta-floured parcels make a delicious lunch served with a salad or as a snack at any time. They are perfect for lunch boxes or food on the go.

FAGOTTINI CON POMODORINI SECCHI E OLIVE
Sun-Dried Tomato and Olive Parcels

Makes 6

7g/¼oz fresh yeast
150ml/5fl oz/⅔ cup lukewarm water
150g/5½oz/scant 1¼ cups strong white bread flour
125g/4½oz/1 cup polenta (cornmeal) flour
1 tsp salt
80g/3oz sun-dried tomatoes, roughly chopped
6 pitted green olives, roughly chopped
a little extra virgin olive oil, for brushing

Line a flat baking tray with parchment paper.

Dissolve the yeast in the lukewarm water. Combine the flours and salt in a large bowl, add the yeast mixture, and mix well into a dough. Knead for 10 minutes, form into a ball, cover with clingfilm and leave to rest in a warm place for 2 hours, or until doubled in size.

Divide the dough into 6 equal pieces, about 80g/3oz each. Roll out each piece on a lightly floured work surface into a roughly oval shape, place the tomatoes and olives in the centre of each, and roll up along the short side. Place the rolls seam side down on the prepared baking tray, cover with a cloth and leave to rest in a warm place for 1 hour.

Preheat the oven to 180°C (fan)/200°C/400°F/Gas mark 6.

Bake in the oven for 20 minutes, brush with a little extra virgin olive oil and continue to bake for a further 10 minutes until lightly golden. Leave to cool slightly and eat warm. It is also good eaten cold.

PAN DOLCI

When I think of *pan dolci*, my taste buds immediately go into action and my mouth waters. I love the aroma, texture and taste of delicate sweet leavened breads like *brioche*, *panettone* and *danubio* – not too sweet or sickly rich, they are perfect to enjoy for breakfast, tea or after meals.

Pan dolci are sweet leavened breads, which have been enriched with eggs, butter and perhaps other ingredients. The dough has a softer, finer texture than bread because the fat weakens the gluten in the flour. For this reason, enriched doughs require a longer kneading and rising time. Because sugar is often added to *pan dolci* and this inhibits yeast growth, these breads are usually made with a much larger quantity of yeast. Most *pan dolci* take a long time to make, but they really are worth the effort and wait. There is nothing nicer than taking a freshly baked batch of brioche out of the oven – the smell, appearance and taste are definitely worth the time spent. To save on labour, I recommend using a freestanding mixer when making *pan dolci*.

Pan dolci are popular all over Italy and many regional varieties exist. Many are seasonal, like the popular *Panettone* and *Pandoro* at Christmas and the *Colomba* at Easter. These seasonal treats are all industrially made now and available not only in Italy but in shops all over the world. In bakeries and cake shops in Italy, artisanally made *pan dolci* are found and these tend to be of a much higher quality than the mass-produced variety. As with bread, *pan dolci*, too, are part of tradition and culture, and most came about as *cucina povera* (poor man's food) where leftover bread dough was enriched with a little sugar or honey. Apparently this is how *panettone* came about at Christmas time when poorer families added a little dried fruit to bread dough as a special sweet treat for this important feast.

This simple, light sweet bread can be eaten at any time. It is delicious toasted and served with jam for breakfast or teatime. It was traditionally made with lard, but to make it lighter, I have added butter. In Tuscany, slices are often dipped into Vin Santo or coffee.

PAN DOLCE TOSCANO
Tuscan Sweet Bread

Serves 6–8

FOR THE DOUGH:
12g/just under ½oz fresh yeast
150ml/5fl oz/⅔ cup lukewarm water
250g/9oz/2 cups plain (all-purpose) flour, plus
   100g/3½oz/scant 1 cup extra when kneading
2 egg yolks
75g/2¾oz/generous ⅓ cup caster (superfine) sugar
50g/1¾oz/3½ tbsp unsalted butter, softened
grated zest of 1 orange
grated zest of 1 lemon
pinch of ground cinnamon
pinch of salt
icing (confectioners') sugar, for dusting

Grease a 20cm/8in round cake tin and line with parchment paper.

Dissolve the yeast in the lukewarm water. Place 250g/9oz/2 cups flour on a work surface, add the yeast mixture and mix into a dough. Knead for 10 minutes, form into a ball, wrap in clingfilm and leave to rest in a warm place for 1 hour, or until doubled in size.

Meanwhile, whisk the egg yolks, sugar and butter together in a bowl until light and creamy. Add the zests, cinnamon and salt.

Place the risen dough on a work surface, flatten with your hands, and gradually work the egg mixture into the dough, gradually adding the extra flour until a soft dough has formed. Place the dough into the prepared tin, cover with a cloth, and rest in a warm place for a further 1 hour.

Preheat the oven to 170°C (fan)/190°C/375°F/Gas mark 5.

Bake in the oven for 30 minutes until golden. Remove from the oven, leave to cool, then tip out of the tin and dust with icing sugar.

Multi-coloured and multi-flavoured, this beautiful brioche bread will surely impress any table at teatime.

TRECCIA COLORATA
Plaited Sweetbread

Serves 12–15

25g/1oz fresh yeast
100ml/3½fl oz/scant ½ cup lukewarm water
500g/1lb 2 oz/4 cups strong white bread flour
10g/¼oz/1½ tsp salt
30g/1oz/2 tbsp caster (superfine) sugar
3 eggs, beaten
70g/2½oz/5 tbsp unsalted butter, melted and cooled
30g/1oz/⅓ cup cocoa powder
30g/1oz dark chocolate chips
grated zest of 1 orange
25ml/1fl oz/2 tbsp orange liqueur
40g/1½oz/scant ½ cup walnuts, roughly chopped
2 pinches of saffron powder,
    diluted in 10ml/2 teaspoons milk
40g/1½oz/scant ¼ cup sultanas (golden raisins),
    soaked in enough rum to cover
icing (confectioners') sugar, for sifting (optional)

Line a large tray with parchment paper and dissolve the yeast in the lukewarm water.

Mix the flour, salt and sugar together in a large bowl. Make a well in the centre and pour in the yeast mixture, eggs and melted butter, and mix well to form a dough. Knead for 5 minutes, then cover with clingfilm and leave to rest in a warm place for 1 hour, or until doubled in size.

Divide the dough into 3 equal pieces, about 275g/9¾oz each. Take one piece and mix in the cocoa powder, chocolate chips, orange zest and suit yourself with the orange liqueur. You may find you need more or less, so add this gradually. Knead until everything is well incorporated, then roll out into a long sausage about 45cm/17¾in in length and set aside.

Take another piece of dough, add the walnuts and saffron mixture and proceed as above.

Take the third piece of dough and add the sultanas. You may find you do not need all the rum, so add this gradually.

Form the 3 sausage shapes into a plait, place on the prepared baking tray, and rest in a warm place for a further 1 hour, or until doubled in size.

Preheat the oven to 180°C (fan)/200°C/400°F/Gas mark 6.

Bake the plait in the oven for 25 minutes. Remove from the oven, leave to cool, then sift with icing sugar, if liked, and serve.

This *pan dolce* (sweet bread) is a typical delicacy of the Tuscan town of Lucca. Its name is taken from the Latin *buccellatum*, meaning mouthful. It was eaten by the ancient Romans. Over time, it has evolved with currants and aniseed. It is usually made into a ring or long sausage shape and is especially popular during the Lucca festivals in September. I was very pleasantly surprised when I first made this cake; not too sweet, a slight aroma of aniseed and packed full of currants, which I love. It's ideal for breakfast or at any time with a coffee.

BUCCELLATO DI LUCCA
Aniseed and Currant Ring Cake

Serves 8

150g/5½oz/scant 1 cup currants
20ml/¾fl oz/4 tsp aniseed liqueur (e.g. Sambuca)
25g/1oz fresh yeast
1 tsp runny honey
160ml/5½fl oz/scant ¾ cup lukewarm water
480g/1lb/4 cups strong white bread flour, sifted
150g/5½oz/¾ cup caster (superfine) sugar
15g/½oz aniseed seeds
1 egg
30g/1oz/2 tbsp unsalted butter, melted and cooled
egg wash (see p.13)

Grease a 24cm/9½in ring tin and line with parchment paper. Soak the currants in the aniseed liqueur, adding enough lukewarm water to cover. Set aside.

Dissolve the yeast and honey in the lukewarm water. Mix the flour, sugar and aniseed seeds together in a large bowl. Add the egg, butter, drained currants and yeast mixture, and mix until well incorporated and a dough is formed. Knead for 2 minutes, then form into a ball, cover with clingfilm, and leave to rest in a warm place for 2 hours, or until doubled in size.

Roll out the dough with your hands on a lightly floured work surface and form into a long sausage shape to fit into the prepared tin, cover with clingfilm, and rest in a warm place for 1½ hours, or until doubled in size.

Preheat the oven to 160°C (fan)/180°C/350°F/Gas mark 4.

Brush the cake with egg wash and bake in the oven for 50 minutes until the top is golden brown. Remove from the oven, leave to cool, then tip out of the tin, slice and serve.

I love *Pandoro* and so does my family, so I had to include this alternative Italian Christmas cake in this book. Unlike *Panettone* (see p.145), it does not contain any dried fruit and often it is preferred for this reason – my daughter, Chloe, would eat *Pandoro* every day if she could! Making *Pandoro* at home does take time, so begin the day before as it needs to rest in the refrigerator overnight as well as rise before and after. The result is certainly worth the effort, ending with a less sweet cake than the industrially produced shop-bought variety. It does dry out quicker than the shop-bought ones, so it's best eaten within a couple of days, however, I don't think that will be a problem, well not in my house anyway!

PANDORO

Serves 10

20g/¾oz fresh yeast
60ml/2¼fl oz/¼ cup lukewarm milk, plus 3 tbsp
125g/4½oz/scant ⅔ cup caster (superfine) sugar
1 egg yolk
480g/1lb/scant 4 cups plain (all-purpose) flour, sifted
3 eggs
170g/6oz/¾ cup unsalted butter, cut into small cubes and softened at room temperature
seeds of 1 vanilla pod (bean)
1 tsp salt
20g/¾oz/4 tsp melted unsalted butter
icing (confectioners') sugar, for dusting

Dissolve 15g/½oz fresh yeast in 60ml/2¼fl oz lukewarm milk. Stir in 25g/1oz/2 tbsp sugar and 1 egg yolk. Add 50g/1¾oz/scant ½ cup flour and stir until it is well incorporated. Cover with clingfilm and leave to rest for about 1 hour, or until it is doubled in volume.

Dissolve the remaining (5g/⅛oz) yeast in 3 tablespoons lukewarm milk. Add this to the above mixture. Stir in the remaining (100g/3½oz/½ cup) sugar and 1 egg. Stir in 200g/7oz/scant 1⅔ cups flour and 30g/1oz/ 2 tbsp butter until it is all well incorporated. Cover with clingfilm and leave to rest for 1 hour, or until it has doubled in volume.

Add the remaining (230g/8oz/scant 2 cups) flour, 2 eggs, sugar, vanilla and salt to the mixture, and mix until everything is well incorporated. Lightly grease a large bowl and place the sticky dough inside it. Cover with clingfilm and leave to rest in a warm place for 1 hour, or until doubled in size, then leave to chill overnight (12–15 hours).

Place the dough on a floured work surface and, using a rolling pin, roll out into a square. Place 140g/5oz/⅔ cup butter cubes into the centre of the dough square and fold over the 4 corners, sealing well so the butter does not escape. Press down with your hands and roll into a rectangular shape. Fold over 3 times, then place on a plate or board, cover with clingfilm and leave to chill for 20 minutes.

Fold the dough over again 3 times, then gently press down and leave to chill for 15 minutes. Repeat the process and leave to chill for a further 15 minutes.

Roll out the dough on a lightly floured work surface into a square. Fold over the 4 corners and form into a ball. Spread a little melted butter all over the ball of dough. With the remaining melted butter, grease a large 8-point star-shaped 750g/1lb 10oz *Pandoro* tin (available online), then place the dough inside, cover with clingfilm and leave to rest in a warm place for about 4 hours, or until the dough has risen to the top of the tin.

Preheat the oven to 150°C (fan)/170°C/325°F/Gas mark 3.

Bake the *Pandoro* on the bottom shelf of the oven at this temperature for 15 minutes. Reduce the oven temperature to 130°C (fan)/150°C/300°F/Gas mark 2, cover the top of the *Pandoro* with foil, and continue to cook for 40 minutes until cooked through. Check by inserting a wooden skewer; if it comes out clean, the cake is cooked, if it is still moist, cook for a little longer.

Remove from the oven, leave to cool, then turn out onto a flat plate and, when completely cold, dust with icing sugar and serve.

The traditional Italian Christmas cake, *Panettone*, although delicious, is quite a lengthy process to make at home. I have therefore come up with this quick way of making the mini version, so often found in coffee shops these days and not always good. Made with fast-action dried yeast and only left to rise once, they are quick and simple to make at any time. They are not too sweet either, so perfect to enjoy with a cappuccino for breakfast.

PANETTONCINI VELOCI
Quick Mini *Panettone*

Makes 10 mini *panettone*

500g/1lb 2oz/4 cups strong white bread flour
pinch of salt
2 x 7g/¼oz sachets of dried yeast
seeds of 1 vanilla pod (bean)
100g/3½oz/½ cup caster (superfine) sugar
3 eggs, beaten
150ml/5fl oz/⅔ cup milk
120g/4oz/½ cup unsalted butter,
    melted and cooled
100g/3½oz/scant ½ cup ricotta, drained
70g/2½oz mixed dried fruit
70g/2½oz/½ cup pine kernels
grated zest of 1 orange
grated zest of 1 lemon

Grease and line 10 mini *panettone* moulds with parchment paper.

Mix the flour, salt, yeast, vanilla and sugar together in a large bowl. Make a well in the centre and stir in the eggs and milk, then add the butter. In a separate bowl, combine the ricotta, dried fruit, pine kernels and citrus zests. Add this to the rest of the ingredients and combine well, beating with your hand. The dough will be sticky but don't worry. Cover with a cloth and leave to rest in a warm place for about 1½ hours, or until doubled in size.

Preheat the oven to 190°C (fan)/200°C/400°F/Gas mark 6.

Place dollops of the mixture into the prepared moulds and bake in the oven for about 25 minutes until golden brown.

Remove from the oven, leave to cool, then turn out of the moulds and enjoy.

There are many varieties of *pan dolce* with dried fruit in every region of Italy and this is my version. It may take a little time to make but it is worth the effort. The addition of mixed tropical fruit cuts through the richness and gives the cake a very pleasant taste. I shape it into a coil to give it variety from the classic ring shape into which a lot of *pan dolci* are made. The smell during cooking is irresistible, but do wait for the cake to cool before serving.

PAN DOLCE ALLA FRUTTA SECCA ESOTICA MISTA

Mixed Tropical Fruit Bread

Serves 10

20g/¾oz fresh yeast
70ml/2½fl oz/3½ tbsp lukewarm milk
600g/1lb 5oz/scant 5 cups strong white bread flour
250g/9oz mixed tropical dried fruit
about 100ml/3½fl oz/scant ½ cup Vin Santo
  (or other sweet wine)
10g/¼oz/1½ tsp salt
130g/4½oz/⅔ cup caster (superfine) sugar
grated zest of 1 lemon
3 eggs
100g/3½oz/7 tbsp unsalted butter, melted and
  slightly cooled
30ml/1fl oz/2 tbsp lukewarm milk

Line a 24cm/9½in round cake tin with parchment paper.

Dissolve the yeast in 70ml/2½fl oz/3½ tbsp of lukewarm milk. Place 100g/3½oz/scant 1 cup of flour in a large bowl, add the yeast liquid and mix into a dough. Form into a ball, cover with clingfilm and leave to rest in a warm place for 1½ hours, or until it has doubled in size.

Place the dried fruit in a small bowl, pour over the Vin Santo and leave to soak.

Place the risen dough, remaining flour, salt, sugar, zest, eggs, melted butter and milk in a large bowl and work into a dough. It will be sticky to start, but continue mixing and kneading. You will find it easier to do this on a lightly floured work surface. Place the dough into the bowl, cover with a cloth, and leave to rise in a warm place for 2 hours, or until doubled in size.

Roll out the dough on a lightly floured work surface into a roughly rectangular shape about 5mm/¼in thick. Scatter the drained dried fruit all over, then roll the dough into a sausage shape, securing well by pressing the dough with your fingers to ensure the filling does not escape. Wrap the large sausage around into a coil shape and carefully place in the lined cake tin. Cover with a cloth and leave in a warm place for a further 1 hour.

Preheat the oven to 190°C (fan)/200°C/400°F/Gas mark 6.

Bake the fruit bread in the oven for 1 hour. If you find the top becomes brown quite quickly, place foil over the top for the duration of baking.

Remove from the oven, leave to cool, then turn out of the tin, slice and enjoy!

The addition of yogurt and olive oil gives this brioche loaf a lovely light texture. It is perfect for breakfast either plain or toasted and especially delicious spread with Nutella. The lack of butter and only a little sugar makes this a very healthy option, and it is so much nicer than the shop-bought variety which I find very sweet. The dough can be made by hand but it will be a little sticky to handle – don't worry, this is perfectly normal. If you prefer, you can make it in a freestanding mixer which will do all the sticky work for you in no time.

PAN BRIOCHE
Brioche Loaf

Serves 4–6

22g/¾oz fresh yeast
100ml/3½fl oz/scant ½ cup lukewarm milk, plus
    extra for brushing
450g/15oz/scant 3⅔ cups strong white bread flour
pinch of salt
40g/1½oz/scant ¼ cup caster (superfine) sugar
120ml/4fl oz/½ cup organic plain yogurt
60ml/2¼fl oz/¼ cup olive oil
2 eggs
1 tsp runny honey
1 tsp vanilla extract
sugar granules, for topping

I used a silicone 900g/2lb loaf tin so I didn't have to grease it, but for other loaf tins, lightly grease with some oil.

Dissolve the yeast in the lukewarm milk.

Mix the flour, salt and sugar together in a large bowl. Add the yogurt, olive oil, eggs, honey, vanilla and yeast mixture, and mix well to form a dough. Cover with clingfilm and leave to rest in a warm place for 4 hours.

Place the dough on a lightly floured work surface and place in the prepared loaf tin. Leave to rest in a warm place for a further 1 hour, or until doubled in size.

Preheat the oven to 170°C (fan)/190°C/375°F/Gas mark 5.

Brush the top of the brioche with a little milk and sprinkle with sugar granules. Bake in the oven for 30 minutes until well risen and golden. Remove from the oven, leave to cool, then tip out of the tin and slice.

This soft, light, sweet brioche is popular in Naples. It originates from Austria and was first made in a Neapolitan pastry shop in the 1920s after the owner married a woman from the Saltzburg region. Authentically known as *Buchteln* and filled with apricot jam, the Italians renamed it *Danubio*. This recipe is filled with a delicious homemade custard cream, but it can also be filled with any jam or pieces of chocolate. It's probably worth making double the quantity, as once you start to eat you can't stop! There is a savoury version on p.50.

DANUBIO DOLCE CON CREMA PASTICCIERA
Sweet Brioche Filled with Custard Cream

Serves 4–6

FOR THE BRIOCHE:
6g/¼oz fresh yeast
115ml/4fl oz/½ cup milk, lukewarm
300g/10½oz/scant 2½ cups strong white bread flour
1 tsp salt
15g/½oz/1 tbsp caster (superfine) sugar
seeds of ½ vanilla pod (bean)
grated zest of 1 lemon
1 egg, beaten
25g/1oz/2 tbsp melted unsalted butter, slightly cooled
egg wash (see p.13)

FOR THE CUSTARD CREAM:
100ml/3½fl oz/scant ½ cup milk
25ml/1fl oz/2 tbsp double (heavy) cream
piece of lemon rind
½ vanilla pod (use the pod/bean from above)
2 egg yolks
20g/¾oz/5 tsp granulated or caster (superfine) sugar
12g/just under ½oz cornflour (cornstarch)

Lightly grease a 20cm/8in round sandwich cake tin and line with parchment paper.

Dissolve the yeast in the lukewarm milk. Mix the flour, salt, sugar, vanilla seeds and zest together in a large bowl. Add the yeast mixture and mix until it is well amalgamated. Add the egg and butter and work into a soft dough. Knead the dough on a lightly floured work surface for about 10 minutes until smooth. Cover with clingfilm and leave to rest in a warm place for 2 hours, or until doubled in size.

Meanwhile, make the custard. Combine the milk, cream, lemon rind and vanilla pod in a small pan and leave to infuse over a gentle heat for about 5 minutes, stirring occasionally.

Beat the egg yolks and sugar together in a bowl until light and fluffy, then beat in the cornflour. Remove the pan from the heat and whisk in the egg mixture. Replace the pan over a low heat and whisk continuously until you obtain a thick creamy consistency. Pour into a bowl or plate, cover with clingfilm and leave to cool.

Divide the dough into 15 pieces weighing about 30g/1oz each. Shape each into a ball, then flatten into small circles with a rolling pin. Place 1 teaspoon of the custard cream into the centre, sealing the edges well and closing to form small balls. Place in the prepared tin, cover with clingfilm and rest in a warm place for a further 1 hour, or until doubled in size.

Preheat the oven to 160°C (fan)/180°C/350°F/Gas mark 4.

Brush egg wash all over the top of the brioche and bake in the oven for 20 minutes until golden brown. Remove from the oven, leave to cool slightly, then tear and share.

Col tuppo in Sicilian dialect means 'putting hair in a bun' and the shape of these brioches is reminiscent of this once traditional hairstyle. These brioches are served all over Sicily in cafés and pastry shops, filled with classic almond granita or ice cream for a delicious summer breakfast. They are delicious enjoyed on their own too with a coffee and are best eaten on the day they are made. Otherwise wrap in clingfilm or foil to keep fresh for a few more days. The rising times are quite long, but it's worth the wait! If you have a freestanding mixer, I suggest you use it for this recipe – it will be much easier to incorporate the butter.

BRIOCHE COL TUPPO
Sicilian Brioche

Makes 6

7g/¼oz fresh yeast
35ml/1fl oz/2 tbsp
   lukewarm milk
250g/9oz/2 cups strong
   white bread flour, sifted
40g/1½oz/scant ¼ cup
   caster (superfine) sugar
6g/¼oz/1 tsp salt
3 eggs
170g/6oz/¾ cup unsalted
   butter, diced and softened
egg wash (see p.13)
good-quality ice cream, to
   serve (optional)

Line a large flat baking tray with parchment paper and dissolve the yeast in the lukewarm milk.

Mix the flour, sugar and salt together in a large bowl or freestanding mixer. Mix in the yeast mixture and the eggs, one at a time, then very gradually mix in the butter, combining well between each addition, otherwise you will get lumps of butter in the mixture. This will take quite a long time, especially if you are beating by hand.

If the mixture has been in the mixer, transfer it to a large bowl, cover with clingfilm and leave to rest in a warm place for 4 hours. After this time, the mixture will have tripled in size. Chill for about 12 hours but no longer than 18 hours. Overnight is best for this.

Place the dough on a lightly floured work surface and, using your hands, roll into a large sausage shape, then divide the dough into 6 equal pieces. Remove a small piece from each portion and roll both pieces into balls. Flatten the larger piece and make an indentation, then place the smaller ball into the indentation. Place the brioches onto the prepared baking tray, brush all over with egg wash and leave to rest in a warm place for a further 2 hours.

Preheat the oven to 160°C (fan)/180°C/350°F/Gas mark 4.

Bake the brioches in the oven for 25 minutes. Remove from the oven and place on a wire rack. If wished, gently tear off the top, fill with ice cream and enjoy!

Dove-shaped breads can be traced back to the ancient Greeks and Egyptians, and biblically the dove has always been a symbol of peace. There are many legends about the origins of this sweet bread, but *Colomba* was first produced industrially in the 1930s by Milanese company, Motta, makers of the famous *Panettone* (see p.145). Wanting to create a similar cake for Easter, this dove-shaped version with candied fruits, topped with almonds, was born and has since become a must-have on the Italian Easter table. This wonderful, delicate sweet bread can of course be enjoyed at any time of the year and the silicone dove-shaped mould can be purchased online. As it is not too sweet, it is delicious eaten for breakfast. It is best eaten freshly made – wrap any leftovers up in foil and keep in an airtight container. The shop-bought ones do last longer, but are not as delicious as this homemade version.

COLOMBA
Dove-Shaped Easter Cake

Makes 1 x cake/Serves 12

FOR THE STARTER DOUGH:
10g/¼oz fresh yeast
120ml/4fl oz/½ cup milk, lukewarm
95g/3½oz/¾ cup plain (all-purpose) flour, sifted
FOR THE CAKE:
13g/½oz fresh yeast
70g/2½oz/generous ⅓ cup caster (superfine) sugar, plus 1 tsp
2 eggs
1 egg yolk
1 tsp vanilla extract
110g/4oz/½ cup unsalted butter, softened, plus extra for greasing
250g/9oz/2 cups plain (all-purpose) flour, sifted
½ tsp salt
grated zest of 1 lemon
grated zest of 1 orange
130g/4½oz good-quality candied peel, diced
FOR THE TOPPING:
30g/1oz/⅓ cup ground almonds
50g/1¾oz/scant ¼ cup caster (superfine) sugar

First, make the starter dough. Dissolve the yeast in the lukewarm milk. Place the flour in a large bowl, add the yeast mixture, and stir with a wooden spoon until it is well incorporated. Cover with clingfilm and leave at room temperature for 12 hours, or overnight.

The next day, mix the yeast and 1 teaspoon sugar together in a small bowl to form a paste. Whisk the eggs and sugar together in a large bowl until light and creamy. Add the yeast mixture and vanilla extract, then add the starter dough and butter, and beat gently with a wooden spoon or spatula until everything is well incorporated. Fold in the flour and salt. Turn out on a lightly floured work surface and knead by hand for 10 minutes. Incorporate the zests and candied fruit, and knead for 1 minute until well amalgamated. Place the dough in a lightly buttered bowl, cover with clingfilm, and rest in a warm place for 2 hours, or until doubled in size.

Carefully place the dough in a 1kg/2lb 4oz silicone dove-shaped baking mould, cover with clingfilm, and leave to rest in a warm place for 1 hour.

Meanwhile, make the topping. Whisk all the ingredients together in a large bowl to form a smooth paste. Set aside.

Preheat the oven to 180°C (fan)/200°C/400°F/Gas mark 6.

Spread the paste all over the top of the dove, scatter the almonds over and sprinkle with a little sifted icing sugar. Place the mould on a flat baking tray and bake in the oven

1 egg white
½ tbsp cornflour (cornstarch)
TO DECORATE:
30g/1oz/scant ¼ cup whole
    almonds
icing (confectioners') sugar

for 15 minutes. Reduce the oven temperature to 160°C (fan)/180°C/350°F/Gas mark 4, cover the dove with foil and continue to bake for a further 15 minutes.

Remove from the oven, leave to cool, then carefully turn the dove out of the mould and place onto a plate or board.

This almond tea bread was meant to be made into a ring shape, but during the testing of the recipe, we found we didn't have quite enough dough, so we changed it into a horseshoe shape which actually looks really nice and different. The ricotta filling adds moisture and the cocoa powder gives it a good colour when cut into slices. It's lovely to enjoy at teatime.

PAN DOLCE MANDORLATO A FORMA DI ZOCCOLO DI CAVALLO

Almond Horseshoe

Serves 6–8

FOR THE DOUGH:
12g/scant ½oz fresh yeast
125ml/4fl oz/½ cup
   lukewarm milk
400g/14oz/scant 1¼ cups
   strong white bread flour
1 tsp salt
70g/2½oz/⅓ cup caster
   (superfine) sugar
1 tsp vanilla extract
grated zest of 1 large orange
1 egg
1 egg yolk
50g/1¾oz/3½ tbsp
   unsalted butter, melted
FOR THE FILLING:
100g/3½oz/scant ½ cup
   ricotta
40g/1½oz/scant ¼ cup
   caster (superfine) sugar
50g/1¾oz/½ cup cocoa
   powder
100g/3½oz amaretti
   biscuits (cookies),
   crushed
100g/3½oz/1 cup flaked
   (slivered) almonds,
   roughly chopped, plus
   extra for sprinkling
1 egg
1 tbsp Marsala
egg wash (see p.13)

Line a large flat baking tray with parchment paper. Dissolve the yeast in the lukewarm milk.

Mix the flour, salt and sugar together in a large bowl. Add the remaining ingredients, including the yeast mixture, and mix into a smooth dough. Knead for 5 minutes, then form into a ball, wrap in clingfilm and leave to rest in a warm place for 1 hour, or until doubled in size.

Meanwhile, make the filling. Mix the ricotta and sugar together in a bowl until creamy. Stir in the cocoa powder until it is well incorporated, then stir in the crushed biscuits, the flaked almonds, egg and Marsala. Cover with clingfilm and leave to chill for about 30 minutes, or until required.

Roll out the dough on a lightly floured work surface into a roughly rectangular shape of about 45 x 30cm/17¾ x 12in or as thin as you can get it. Spread the filling all over leaving a small border of about 4cm/1½in. Carefully roll from the long side, sealing the edges well with the help of a little water. Form into a horseshoe shape and make small incisions with a sharp knife around the side. Carefully place on the prepared baking tray and leave to rest in a warm place for a further 30 minutes.

Preheat the oven to 180°C (fan)/200°C/400°F/Gas mark 6.

Brush with egg wash, scatter with extra flaked almonds and bake in the oven for about 30 minutes until golden all over. If it starts to brown before the end of cooking time, cover with foil. Leave to cool before eating.

Buondi means 'good day' – what a fabulous name for the Italian equivalent of morning croissants! These remind me of my youth when every café in Italy would sell them for breakfast. Nowadays you can buy industrially produced *buondi* in shops in Italy, but the taste and smell of baking them at home is beyond comparison! They are not difficult to make, but their resting time is long, so begin the day before, and if you want them freshly made for a breakfast treat it will be an early morning start!

BUONDÌ
Italian Croissants

Makes 20

FOR THE STARTER:
10g/¼oz fresh yeast
55ml/1¾fl oz/scant ¼ cup lukewarm water
100g/3½oz/scant 1 cup strong white bread flour
FOR THE MIXTURE:
100g/3½oz/½ cup caster (superfine) sugar
80ml/3fl oz/5 tbsp milk
2 tsp runny honey
8 egg yolks
400g/14oz/scant 3¼ cups strong white bread flour
200g/7oz/scant 1 cup unsalted butter, softened
grated zest of 1 lemon
grated zest of 1 orange
2 drops of orange water essence
seeds of 1 vanilla pod (bean)
10g/¼oz/1½ tsp salt
FOR THE SYRUP:
100ml/3½fl oz/scant ½ cup water
150g/5½oz/¾ cup granulated or
   caster (superfine) sugar
sugar granules, for topping

The day before, make the starter dough. Dissolve the yeast in lukewarm water. Put the flour in a large bowl, add the yeast mixture and mix to a smooth dough. Form the dough into a ball, cover with clingfilm, and leave to rest in a warm place for 1 hour.

Mix the sugar, honey and milk together in a large bowl. In a separate bowl, whisk the egg yolks until creamy, then gradually add them to the sugar mixture, alternating with flour until everything is well incorporated. Add the butter (if necessary give the butter a quick whisk so it is soft

and gooey), citrus zests, orange water essence, vanilla, salt and starter dough, and mix well by hand for about 10 minutes until everything is well incorporated. Cover with clingfilm and leave to rest in a warm place for 2 hours. After this time, leave the dough to chill for 12 hours.

The next day, divide the dough into 20 pieces roughly weighing 50g/1¾oz each. Shape into small fat sausages about 7cm/2¾in long and 4.5cm/1¾in wide, and place in individual small loaf tins. Leave to rest in a warm place for 4 hours.

Preheat the oven to 160°C (fan)/180°C/350°F/Gas mark 4.

Bake the *buondi* in the oven for about 15 minutes until golden brown, then remove from the oven and leave to cool.

Meanwhile, make the syrup. Bring the water and sugar to the boil in a small saucepan for about 1 minute until sugar has dissolved. Remove from the heat and leave to cool slightly.

Remove the *buondi* from the tins and place on a wire rack. Brush with the cooled syrup and top with sugar granules.

CROSTATE

Crostate are the sweet tarts which to many Italians, including myself, evoke happy childhood memories. Traditionally home baked by mamma or nonna, filled with homemade jam and topped with criss-crossed strips of pastry, it was always a welcome teatime treat.

Pasta frolla (shortcrust pastry) is generally used as a basis for most sweet tarts. Basic ingredients of flour, butter, sugar and egg yolks are used to make this popular rich and sweet pastry. Italians have over the years evolved their approach to pastry, and puff pastry as well as filo are popular choices for many desserts. I normally like to make all my own pastry; however, I do make an exception when it comes to the latter as they are quite labour intensive. As with bread, Italians are now experimenting with different grains, and pastries made from buckwheat or spelt or rice flour are not uncommon.

Pasta frolla is really simple to make, and if you make it in a freestanding mixer, it is even quicker. As soon as the dough is ready, make sure you wrap it tightly in clingfilm and leave it to rest and cool down in the refrigerator for at least 30 minutes. When I make pastry, I like to make a large quantity so I can freeze what I don't need and use it to make another *crostata* at another time.

Fillings vary, too, including the classic *Crostata di Marmellata* (Jam Tart, see p.169) and the *Crostata di Ricotta e Nutella* (Ricotta and Nutella Tart, see p.161). Ricotta is used a lot in Italian desserts and *crostate* are no exception as it provides an excellent filling, combining well with other ingredients, and is also less fatty than cream. *Crema pasticciera* (custard cream) is another favourite filling which is homemade and often flavoured with lemon or chocolate, depending on your *crostata*. Italians love fruit so fruit-topped *crostate* in season are a popular choice.

TIPS FOR MAKING PASTRY:

• Work in a cool, dry kitchen.

• Use good-quality butter or other fat as the taste of the fat will affect the flavour of the pastry.

• Work quickly and lightly; overworked pastry can be tough.

• When rolling out the dough, use only a little flour to dust the work surface as any additional flour can make the dough dry.

• Always leave your dough to rest in the refrigerator.

• **BAKING BLIND** means to cook the pastry case before adding any filling. When you have lined the tart tin with the dough, place a circle of parchment paper a little larger than the diameter of the pastry case and place over the dough. Top with a layer of ceramic baking beans or dried beans and bake in the preheated oven for about 15 minutes, then carefully remove the beans and parchment paper and continue to bake for a further 5 minutes or so until the pastry case becomes golden.

There is nothing nicer than the taste of homemade custard. It is so much more nutritious and less sweet than the bought variety and is also so simple to make. *Crema pasticciera* is widely used in Italy for a lot of desserts and cakes in preference to cream. This is my sister Adriana's recipe, which forms the basis of custard fillings for the tarts in this book.

CREMA PASTICCIERA FATTA IN CASA
Thick Homemade Custard

Makes enough to fill the pastry cases in the book

500ml/18fl oz/2 cups whole milk
seeds of 1 vanilla pod (bean)
6 egg yolks
100g/3½oz/½ cup granulated or
   caster (superfine) sugar
60g/2¼oz/½ cup plain (all-purpose) flour, sifted

Place the milk and vanilla seeds in a small saucepan over a medium heat until the milk is hot but not boiling.

Meanwhile, whisk the egg yolks and sugar together in a bowl until light and fluffy. Gradually add the flour and continue to whisk until it is incorporated. Pour in the hot milk and continue to whisk for a few seconds – make sure there are no lumps – if there are, continue to whisk until they have disappeared.

Return the mixture to the pan over a medium heat and heat stirring constantly with a wooden spoon until the custard begins to thicken. At this point, increase the heat and stir quickly, but do not allow it to boil or burn. If this happens, take the pan immediately off the heat.

To allow the custard to cool quicker, pour it into a heatproof bowl or container, cover with a lid or clingfilm and leave to cool.

Ricotta is a very popular filling in Italy for both sweet and savoury pies and tarts. Lighter than a lot of other creamy cheeses, it is ideal used in desserts. I find ricotta especially delicious combined with chocolate, hence the idea of adding a thin layer of Nutella – the ricotta cuts through the sweetness and makes for a really yummy tart. It is lovely to serve as a dessert or simply at teatime.

CROSTATA DI RICOTTA E NUTELLA
Ricotta and Nutella Tart

Serves 6

FOR THE PASTRY:
250g/9oz/2 cups plain (all-purpose) flour, sifted
pinch of salt
125g/4½oz/½ cup cold unsalted butter, cut into small pieces
100g/3½oz/½ cup caster (superfine) sugar
2 egg yolks
FOR THE FILLING:
400g/14oz/1¾ cups ricotta
1 tbsp granulated or caster (superfine) sugar
1 tbsp Marsala or other sweet wine
50g/1¾oz milk chocolate, roughly chopped (optional)
½ small jar (about 100g/3½oz) of Nutella

To make the pastry, combine the flour and salt in a large bowl. Add the butter and rub it in until it resembles breadcrumbs. Add sugar, then add the egg yolks and mix well to form a smooth dough. Wrap in clingfilm and leave to chill for at least 30 minutes.

Meanwhile, preheat the oven to 160°C (fan)/180°C/350°F/ Gas mark 4. Grease a 24cm/9½in round tart tin with a little melted butter, then dust with flour.

For the filling, mix the ricotta, sugar, Marsala and chocolate pieces, if using, together in a bowl. Cover with clingfilm and leave to chill until required.

Roll out the dough on a lightly floured work surface to a thickness of 5mm/¼in and use to line the prepared tart tin. Trim off the excess pastry and set aside. Spread a thin layer of Nutella over the bottom of the pastry case followed by the ricotta mixture. Reroll the remaining pastry and cut into strips. Place over the top of the tart, making a lattice pattern.

Bake in the oven for 40 minutes until golden. Eat warm or leave to cool.

This is a lovely rustic tart made with dried apricots, which are cooked to make a jam. It reminds me of the homemade *crostata* made by family and friends when I was growing up in Italy. An extra layer of the unsweetened pastry is added in the middle to cut through the sweetness of the apricot filling. You can substitute the apricots with prunes and use walnuts or flaked almond instead of pine kernels, if you prefer.

CROSTATA DI ALBICOCCHE SECCHE
Dried Apricot Tart

Serves 6

FOR THE PASTRY:
1 egg
2 egg yolks
350g/12oz/scant 3 cups plain (all-purpose) flour, sifted
pinch of salt
140g/5oz/scant ⅔ cup cold unsalted butter, cut into small pieces
FOR THE FILLING:
250g/9oz/scant 1½ cups dried apricots
180g/6oz/scant 1 cup caster (superfine) sugar
juice of ½ lemon
grated zest of 1 lemon
45g/1½oz/⅓ cup pine kernels
egg wash (see p.13)

Soak the dried apricots for the filling in enough lukewarm water to cover.

To make the pastry, beat the egg and yolks together and set aside. Mix the flour and salt in a large bowl, add the butter and rub it in until it resembles breadcrumbs. Add the eggs and mix well to form a smooth pastry. Form into a ball, wrap in clingfilm and leave to chill until required.

Meanwhile, make the filling. Drain the apricots and place the water into a saucepan together with the sugar and stir over a low heat until the sugar has dissolved. Add the apricots, increase the heat, bring to the boil and cook over a medium-high heat for about 25 minutes, or until it is a jam-like consistency. Remove from the heat and stir in the lemon juice and zest.

Preheat the oven to 160°C (fan)/180°C/350°F/Gas mark 4.

Divide the pastry into 3 pieces, making one slightly larger. Roll out the larger piece on a lightly floured work surface and use to line a 20cm/8in pie dish. Fill with half of the apricot filling and sprinkle with half of the pine kernels. Roll out another piece of dough the same size as the base of the pie dish and place this pastry round over the apricots. Fill with the remaining apricot mixture and sprinkle with the remaining pine kernels. With the remaining pastry, cut out strips with a pastry cutter and form a lattice shape over the top. Carefully fold over any excess pastry which is overhanging around the edge. Brush the pastry all over with egg wash and bake in the oven for about 45 minutes, or until golden.

Remove from the oven, leave to cool, then remove from the pie dish and serve.

I love semolina pudding, which forms the filling of this sophisticated peach tart. You can use other fruit such as strawberries or a selection like mixed berries, kiwi fruit, pineapple, plums or whatever you prefer. This tart makes a lovely dinner party dessert. *Illustrated overleaf.*

CROSTATA DI CREMA DI SEMOLINA E PESCHE
Tart with Semolina Cream and Peaches

Serves 6–8

FOR THE PASTRY:
100g/3½oz/scant 1 cup
    plain (all-purpose) flour
100g/3½oz/scant 1 cup
    rice flour
100g/3½oz/7 tbsp cold
    unsalted butter, cut into
    small pieces
40g/1½oz/scant ¼ cup
    caster (superfine) sugar
1 egg
FOR THE FILLING:
20g/¾oz gelatine leaves
1 litre/1¾ pints/4 cups milk
1 vanilla pod (bean), split in
    half lengthways
100g/3½oz/½ cup
    semolina
100g/3½oz/½ cup
    granulated or caster
    (superfine) sugar
200ml/7fl oz/scant 1 cup
    double (heavy) cream
about 5–6 ripe peaches,
    finely sliced
icing (confectioners') sugar,
    sifted, for sprinkling

First, make the pastry. Sift the flours into a large bowl, add the butter, and rub it in until it resembles breadcrumbs. Stir in the sugar, then add the egg, and mix well to form a smooth dough. Form into a bowl, wrap in clingfilm and leave to chill for at least 30 minutes.

Preheat the oven to 160°C (fan)/180°C/350°F/Gas mark 4.

Roll out the dough on a lightly floured work surface to a thickness of about 3mm/⅛in and use to line a 22cm/8½in loose-bottomed tart tin. Bake blind (see p.159) for about 20 minutes. Remove from the oven, leave to cool, then carefully remove from the tin and place on a flat plate.

Meanwhile, make the filling. Soften the gelatine leaves in enough warm water to just cover. Place the milk and vanilla pod into a saucepan and bring to the boil. Stir in the semolina, reduce the heat and cook for 10 minutes, stirring constantly. Add the sugar and stir until dissolved. Strain the gelatine leaves and add to the mixture. Leave to cool, then remove the vanilla pod. Whisk the cream until stiff and fold it into the semolina mixture.

Pour the mixture into the pastry case, arrange the sliced peaches on top, and sift with icing sugar. Serve.

This lovely strawberry tart looks very pretty and the combination of lemon and strawberries is delicious. It is perfect to make in late spring/early summer when English strawberries are in abundance and at their best. *Illustrated overleaf.*

CROSTATA DI FRAGOLE E LIMONE
Strawberry and Lemon Tart

Serves 8

FOR THE PASTRY:
250g/9oz/2 cups plain (all-purpose) flour, sifted
pinch of salt
125g/4½oz/½ cup cold unsalted butter
80g/3oz/scant ¾ cup icing (confectioners') sugar, sifted, plus extra for sprinkling
grated zest of 1 lemon
2 egg yolks, slightly beaten
FOR THE FILLING:
1 quantity of Thick Homemade Custard (see p.160)
grated zest of 1 lemon
600g/1lb 5oz/scant 4¼ cups strawberries, sliced or left whole depending on size

First, make the pastry. Mix the flour and salt together in a large bowl, add the butter, and rub it in until it resembles breadcrumbs. Stir in the icing sugar and lemon zest, then add the egg yolks and mix well to form a smooth pastry. Form into a ball, wrap in clingfilm, and leave to chill for at least 30 minutes.

Preheat the oven to 160°C (fan)/180°C/350°F/Gas mark 4.

Make the filling. Make the custard according to the recipe on p.160, adding the lemon zest.

Roll out the pastry on a lightly floured work surface and use to line a 22cm/8½in tart tin. Bake blind (see p.159) for about 25 minutes. Remove from the oven and leave to cool, then remove from the tin and carefully place on a flat plate.

Fill the cooked pastry case with the cooled custard and decorate with strawberries and a sprinkling of sifted icing sugar over the top.

These pretty tarts are fun to make and you can use your imagination when it comes to decorating them – in fact, get the kids involved, they will love it! I like to use a selection of jam – apricot, raspberry, plum, peach – or whatever I have in the cupboard. Homemade jam is best, otherwise go for a good-quality brand that does not contain too much sugar!

CROSTATINE DI MARMELLATA
Jam Tarts

Makes 6

FOR THE PASTRY:
250g/9oz/2 cups plain (all-purpose) flour
125g/4½oz/½ cup cold unsalted butter, cut into
    small pieces
75g/2¾oz/generous ⅔ cup icing (confectioners')
    sugar
seeds of ½ vanilla pod (bean)
2 egg yolks
jam of your choice or a selection
egg wash (see p.13)

Sift the flour into a large bowl, add the butter and rub it in until it resembles breadcrumbs. Stir in the icing sugar and vanilla, then add the egg yolks and mix to a smooth dough, working quickly to avoid the dough getting warm. Form the dough into a ball, wrap in clingfilm and leave to chill for at least 30 minutes, or until required.

Preheat the oven to 160°C (fan)/180°C/350°F/Gas mark 4. Lightly grease 6 round 12cm/4½in diameter loose-based tartlet tins with butter, then dust with flour.

Roll out the dough on a lightly floured work surface to a thickness of 5mm/¼in and use to line the prepared tartlet tins. Lightly prick the bottoms with a fork and fill each with jam. Gather up the remaining bits of pastry, roll out, and cut out strips or shapes to place over the top. Brush with a little egg wash.

Place the tins on a flat baking tray and bake in the oven for 20–25 minutes until golden.

Remove from the oven, leave to cool, and carefully remove from the tins.

Like puff pastry, filo is another type of pastry which I don't normally make at home. It takes time and I find the shop-bought one absolutely fine to use. This extremely simple but delicious dessert will surely impress your guests. The thick homemade custard goes really well with the berries. Use whatever is in season and what you prefer.

CROSTATA AI FRUTTI DI BOSCO E CREMA PASTICCIERA

Filo Pastry Tart with Custard and Mixed Berries

Serves 4–6

1 quantity of Thick Homemade Custard (see p.160)
6 square sheets ready-made filo (phyllo) pastry,
    about 24 x 24cm/9½ x 9½in
40g/1½oz/3 tbsp unsalted butter, melted
100g/3½oz/scant ¾ cup mixed fruits of the forest
    (such as raspberries, blueberries, blackberries)

Make the custard according to the recipe on p.160 and leave to cool.

Preheat the oven to 170°C (fan)/190°C/375°F/Gas mark 5. Grease a 20cm/8in sandwich cake tin with some melted butter.

Trim the filo pastry to about 24 x 24cm/9½ x 9½in, if necessary. Line the prepared cake tin with a sheet of filo pastry, leaving any excess pastry hanging down. Brush the sheet with melted butter, then place another sheet of filo over it and brush with melted butter. Continue doing this until you have used up all the sheets.

Pour the cooled custard inside, then arrange the berries all over, pressing down gently into the custard.

Bake in the oven for 30–35 minutes until the pastry becomes a golden brown and the custard is slightly golden.

Remove from the oven, leave to cool, then serve.

This lovely lemon tart has the added kick of limoncello liqueur, making it an ideal dessert when having guests round for dinner. The grated dark chocolate at the end combines really well with the lemon – in fact, where I come from on the Amalfi Coast, it is quite common to find limoncello-filled chocolates, which are delicious! Serve with a glass of cold limoncello for the perfect after-dinner treat.

CROSTATA ALLA CREMA DI LIMONCELLO CON CIOCCOLATO

Creamy Limoncello Tart with Grated Chocolate

Serves 8

FOR THE PASTRY:
250g/9oz/2 cups plain (all-purpose) flour, sifted
pinch of salt
125g/4½oz/½ cup cold unsalted butter
80g/3oz/scant ¾ cup icing (confectioners') sugar, sifted, plus extra for sprinkling
grated zest of 1 lemon
2 egg yolks, slightly beaten

FOR THE FILLING:
1 quantity of Thick Homemade Custard (see p.160)
40ml/1½fl oz/3 tbsp limoncello liqueur
grated zest of 1 large lemon
dark chocolate (at least 70% cocoa solids), for grating

First, make the pastry. Mix the flour and salt in a large bowl, add the butter, and rub it in until it resembles breadcrumbs. Stir in the icing sugar and lemon zest, then add the egg yolks and mix well to form a smooth dough. Form into a ball, wrap in clingfilm and leave to chill for at least 30 minutes.

Preheat the oven to 180°C (fan)/200°C/400°F/Gas mark 6. Grease a tin 22cm/8½in tart tin with some melted butter, then dust with flour.

Make the filling. First, make the custard according to the recipe on p.160. When you take the custard off the heat, stir in the limoncello and lemon zest, then leave to cool.

Roll the pastry out on a lightly floured work surface to a thickness of about 5mm/¼in and use to line the prepared tart tin. Bake blind for about 20–25 minutes. (First 15 minutes with beans, then without, see Pastry Tips on p.159.) Remove from the oven and allow the pastry case to cool. Carefully remove the cooled pastry from the tin and place on a flat plate or board.

Fill the pastry case with the limoncello custard, then grate over the chocolate and serve immediately or chill until required. Serve at room temperature.

These traditional Sardinian Easter pastries, also known as *formagelle* or *casadinas*, depending on region, are filled with ricotta or other local cheese. They are normally made with a pastry using flour, lard and water, however, I prefer them with a rich shortcrust pastry like this one. The pastry can be a little crumbly while preparing it, so work quickly – if you find it too crumbly, place it in the refrigerator for a few minutes to harden before continuing. If you prefer, you can place them directly in small tartlet tins, but the handmade little baskets they resemble are really very pretty and unusual. Delicate and not so sweet, they are perfect if you don't have a sweet tooth. .

PERDULAS
Sardinian Ricotta Tartlets

Makes 8–10 tartlets

FOR THE PASTRY:
250g/9oz/2 cups plain (all-purpose) flour, sifted
140g/5oz/⅔ cup cold unsalted butter, cut into
   small pieces
1 large egg yolk, mixed with 2 tbsp ice-cold water
FOR THE FILLING:
250g/9oz/scant 1 cup ricotta
pinch of salt
1 large egg
40g/1½oz/scant ¼ cup caster (superfine) sugar
10g/¼oz/2 tsp semolina
grated zest of ½ lemon
grated zest of ½ orange
pinch of saffron powder

First, make the pastry. Place the flour into a bowl, add the butter and rub it in until it resembles breadcrumbs. Add the egg yolk mixture, quickly mixing in with your hands to form a dough, adding a little more ice-cold water, if necessary. Form the pastry into a ball or flatten into a disc, wrap in clingfilm and leave to chill for about 30 minutes.

Preheat the oven to 200°C (fan)/220°C/425°F/Gas mark 7. Line a large baking tray with parchment paper.

Meanwhile, make the filling. Place the ricotta in a bowl and mash it lightly with a fork. Stir in a pinch of salt, the egg, sugar, semolina, zests and saffron powder until everything is well incorporated. Cover and chill until required.

Roll out the pastry on a lightly floured work surface to a thickness of about 1cm/½in. Using a 11cm/4¼in in diameter round pastry cutter, cut out circles. Place a circle in the palm of your hand, then place 2 tablespoons of the filling mixture in the centre. With your other hand, pinch the sides all around so the filling does not escape and the tartlet resembles a little basket. Carefully place on the prepared baking tray or inside small tartlet tins and bake in the oven for 20 minutes until well risen and golden brown.

Remove from the oven, leave to cool and enjoy!

For the Neapolitans, these pies are made during Easter symbolising rebirth and fertility – a myth which dates back to pagan times when Neapolitans offered the fruits of the land to the mermaid *Partenope* – eggs for fertility, wheat from the land, ricotta from the shepherds. The recipe has evolved over the years and is now made not only at home but in pastry shops all over the region of Campania during Easter. I usually make a selection of larger pies and small ones like these for family and friends to enjoy at this time of year. The pre-cooked wheat can be found in good Italian delis.

PASTIERINE DI GRANO
Mini Wheat and Ricotta Pies

Makes 6

FOR THE PASTRY:
300g/10½oz/scant 2⅕ cups plain (all-purpose) flour
120g/4oz/½ cup cold unsalted butter,
    cut into pieces
120g/4oz/scant ⅔ cup caster (superfine) sugar
2 large egg yolks
grated zest of 1 orange
egg wash (see p.13)
FOR THE FILLING:
300g/10½oz pre-cooked wheat
    (sold in jars in Italian delis or online)
120ml/4fl oz/½ cup whole milk
15g/½oz/1 tbsp butter
1 tsp ground cinnamon
300g/10½oz/1¼ cups ricotta
seeds of ½ vanilla pod (bean)
200g/7oz/1 cup caster (superfine) sugar
grated zest of 1 orange
1 tbsp orange flower essence
2 eggs
1 egg yolk
FOR THE CREAM:
150ml/5fl oz/⅔ cup whole milk
¼ vanilla pod (bean), split in half lengthways
2 egg yolks
60g/2¼oz/scant ⅓ cup caster (superfine) sugar
15g/½oz/1 tbsp cornflour (cornstarch)

>>

First, make the pastry. Sift the flour into a large bowl, add the butter and rub it in until it resembles breadcrumbs. Stir in the sugar and orange zest, then add the egg yolks and mix to form a smooth pastry. You may need to add a little cold water, but very gradually, just a couple of drops at a time until the dough forms. Form into a ball and wrap in clingfilm. Leave to chill for at least 30 minutes.

Meanwhile, make the filling. Place the wheat, milk, butter and cinnamon in a small saucepan and gently bring to the boil, stirring until the milk has been absorbed. Remove from the heat and set aside to cool.

Make the cream. Place the milk in a saucepan with the vanilla pod and bring almost to boiling point, then remove from the heat. Meanwhile, whisk the egg yolks and sugar together in a heatproof bowl until light and creamy. Stir in the cornflour and whisk until smooth. Gradually pour in the hot milk, whisking all the time to avoid lumps forming. When everything is well incorporated, pour back into the pan and return to a medium heat, stirring constantly until it begins to bubble. Remove and leave to cool.

Whisk the ricotta, vanilla seeds, sugar, orange zest and orange essence into the cooled wheat mixture. Gradually add the eggs and yolks, then stir in the cream and mix well together. Set aside.

Preheat the oven to 160°C (fan)/180°C/350°F/Gas mark 4.

Roll the dough out on a lightly floured work surface to a thickness of about 5mm/¼in and use to line 6 loose-bottomed tartlet tins, about 12cm/4½in in diameter, Lightly prick the bottoms with a fork, then fill each with the creamy mixture. Gather up the remaining bits of pastry, roll out, and cut out thin strips and arrange them criss-cross over the filling. Brush with a little egg wash. Place on a large flat baking tray and bake in the oven for 45 minutes until golden brown.

Remove from the oven, leave to cool, then dust with icing sugar.

This nutritious pumpkin tart is influenced by the American pumpkin pie with the Italian addition of creamy mascarpone cheese. Pumpkin is widely used in Italy, especially for savoury dishes like pasta, risotto, and it is added to stews and used to fill ravioli. Pumpkin is slightly sweet so it is ideal to use in desserts; I remember once during autumn when I had an abundance of pumpkins making a crumble with them which went down really well at my restaurant. I think with the American influence of Halloween in Italy these days, sweet pumpkin dishes such as these are becoming increasingly popular.

CROSTATA DI ZUCCA
Pumpkin Tart

Serves 6

FOR THE PASTRY:
250g/9oz/2 cups plain (all-purpose) flour, sifted
pinch of salt
125g/4½oz/½ cup cold unsalted butter, cut into small pieces
100g/3½oz/½ cup caster (superfine) sugar
2 egg yolks, lightly beaten
FOR THE FILLING:
400g/14oz pumpkin or butternut squash (weight without skin and seeds)
180g/6oz/generous ¾ cup mascarpone cheese
30g/1oz/2 tbsp soft brown sugar
pinch of ground cinnamon
pinch of grated nutmeg
1 tbsp Marsala

To make the pastry, mix the flour and salt together in a large bowl, add the butter and rub it into the flour until it resembles breadcrumbs. Stir in the sugar, then add the egg yolks and mix well to form a pastry. Wrap in clingfilm and leave to chill for about 30 minutes.

Preheat the oven to 180°C (fan)/200°C/400°F/Gas mark 6.

Cut the pumpkin into thin slices, place on a baking tray and bake in the oven for about 30 minutes until softened. Remove, place in a bowl and mash to a soft pulp. Leave to cool, then stir in the mascarpone, sugar, cinnamon, nutmeg and Marsala until everything is well incorporated.

Reduce the oven temperature to 160°C/325°F/Gas mark 3. Grease a 24cm/9½in round tart tin with a little melted butter, then dust with flour.

Roll the dough out on a lightly floured work surface to a thickness of 5mm/¼in and use to line the prepared tart tin. Trim off the excess pastry and set aside. Fill the pastry case with the pumpkin mixture. Reroll the excess pastry, cut into thin strips and place in a lattice pattern over the top of the filling. Bake in the oven for 30 minutes until the pastry is golden.

Remove from the oven, and cool before slicing and serving.

This traditional Austrian dessert is also common in the northern Italian regions of Trentino Alto-Adige and Veneto, whose borders neighbour Austria. It is often made with ready-made filo pastry, but in this recipe I have given you the typical pastry made in Alto Adige. Simple to make, the trick is to get it as thin as you can when rolling it out. The addition of breadcrumbs helps to bind the filling and soak up the juices during baking. It can be enjoyed warm as a dessert with some custard or ice cream and is delicious eaten cold with afternoon tea.

STRUDEL DI MELE
Apple Strudel

Serves 6–8

FOR THE PASTRY:
125g/4½oz/1 cup plain (all-purpose) flour, sifted
pinch of salt
1 egg
1 tbsp extra virgin olive oil
40ml/1½fl oz/3 tbsp lukewarm water

FOR THE FILLING:
40g/1½oz mixed dried fruit, soaked in enough lukewarm water to cover
100g/3½oz/7 tbsp unsalted butter
75g/2¾oz/½ cup dried breadcrumbs
600g/1lb 5oz Golden Delicious apples, peeled, cored and thinly sliced
1 tsp ground cinnamon
grated zest of 1 lemon
50g/1¾oz/¼ cup caster (superfine) sugar
35g/1¼oz/⅓ cup walnuts, roughly chopped
icing (confectioners') sugar, for sprinkling

To make the pastry, place the flour and salt in a large bowl, add the egg, olive oil and lukewarm water, and mix into a fairly sticky dough. Place on a lightly floured work surface and knead gently for a minute or so, adding a little more flour if required, until well incorporated. Form into a ball. Lightly grease a bowl, place the dough ball into it, cover with clingfilm and leave in a cool place for 30 minutes.

Preheat the oven to 180°C (fan)/200°C/400°F/Gas mark 6. Line a flat baking tray with parchment paper.

For the filling, melt 50g/1¾oz/3½ tbsp of butter in a small pan, add the breadcrumbs and stir-fry over a medium heat until toasted and golden brown. Be careful not to burn! Remove from the heat and leave to cool.

Drain the mixed fruit well and combine with the apples, cinnamon, zest and sugar. Stir in the cooled breadcrumbs.

Place a clean cloth or tea towel on the work surface and lightly dust with flour. Place the pastry on top and roll out to a rectangular shape, about 40 x 35cm/16 x 14in, or as thin as you can get it. If the pastry is too sticky, dust with a little flour.

Melt the remaining butter and brush some of it over the pastry, leaving a border of about 2cm/¾in. Arrange the apple mixture over this and top with the chopped walnuts. With the help of the cloth, roll into a long sausage shape, sealing the ends to avoid the filling from escaping and place on the prepared tray. Brush the top with more melted butter and bake in the oven for 30 minutes until slightly golden.

Remove from the oven and leave to cool slightly before sprinkling with icing sugar and slicing.

BISCOTTI

Biscotti (biscuits), as the name suggests, means double-baked as traditionally this is how they were made. In fact, early biscuits were slices of bread that were re-baked in the oven to make them crispy and last longer. Known as *pan biscotto*, they were dunked in water or milk to soften for ease of eating. These types of biscuit were made for sailors to consume during long voyages or were given to soldiers away at war.

In Medieval times, the art of biscuit making was perfected in convents and monasteries, which has shaped the way biscuits are made in Italy today. In the village of Erice in Sicily, a young girl named Maria Grammatico entered the convent in the 1940s and was taught how to bake by the nuns; she perfected this skill and eventually left the convent to open her own shop in the village – the shop is still there and famous for its almond biscuits, attracting locals and tourists from far and wide.

From about the mid-1800s, biscuits were being produced commercially and it was during this era that Davide Lazzaroni set up his famous biscuit empire selling biscuits in beautifully decorated tin boxes. I remember seeing boxes like this at home in Italy and when the biscuits were all eaten, the box would always remain and be used for storing other biscuits or for other household purposes. *Lazzaroni* is still a famous name among Italian biscuit producers and exports all over the world. Probably the best known outside of Italy are the *Amaretti di Saronno* sold in the traditional red boxes.

Of course biscuits we love and enjoy today evolved over the ages with the introduction of new and exciting ingredients and methods of production. Chocolate-covered biscuits or biscuits sandwiched together with various fillings appeared in the last 50 years or so.

As with all Italian food, biscuits, too, vary from region to region. Probably one of the most renowned is the Tuscan *Cantuccini* – known outside of Italy as *biscotti* – and these are still baked twice to achieve a crispy texture. The soft, sponge-like *Savoiardi* from Piemonte have age-old roots and are said to have originally been made for royalty. In the Naples area, rich and spicy honey *Mostaccioli* and *Rococo* biscuits are popular. And in Sicily, almond-based biscuits, often sold in different colours and decorated with candied fruit, are a joy to look at and eat.

These simple biscuits are just the best! They are so moreish that once you start to eat one, you can't stop; the dough is so delicate that the biscuits just melt in your mouth. I like to add vanilla, but you can add other flavourings if you prefer, such as lemon or orange zest. I use a round cutter, but you can make them into lots of different and interesting shapes – my girls love to experiment! They are also a great basis for my Jam or Nutella biscuits, see opposite and p.184.

BASIC BISCUITS

Makes 22 biscuits

150g/5½oz/1¼ cups plain (all-purpose) flour
100g/3½oz/7 tbsp cold unsalted butter, cut into
    small chunks
70g/2½oz/⅔ cup icing (confectioners') sugar, sifted
seeds of ½ vanilla pod (bean)
1 egg yolk

Sift the flour into a bowl, add the butter and rub it in until it resembles breadcrumbs. Mix in the icing sugar and vanilla seeds. Add the egg yolk and work into a smooth dough, working quickly to avoid the dough getting warm. Form the dough into a ball, wrap in clingfilm, and leave to chill for at least 30 minutes, or until required.

Preheat the oven to 170°C (fan)/190°C/375°F/Gas mark 5. Line a flat baking tray with parchment paper.

Roll out the dough on a lightly floured work surface to a thickness of about 5mm/¼in. Using a 5cm/2in round pastry cutter, cut out circles and place onto the prepared baking tray. Bake in the oven for about 10 minutes until lightly golden.

Remove from the oven, leave to cool and enjoy! Store in an airtight container for up to a week.

These popular jam biscuits can be found in bakeries and cake shops all over Italy and made in various shapes and sizes. They are really simple to make at home and fun to make with the children, who will love them! If you can, use homemade or good-quality jam.

BISCOTTI CON LA MARMELLATA
Jam Biscuits

Makes about 12 biscuits

1 quantity of Basic Biscuit dough (see opposite)
jam of your choice, such as strawberry, raspberry or
    apricot, sieved
a little caster (superfine) sugar, for sprinkling

Make the Basic Biscuits according to the recipe opposite. Leave to chill for 30 minutes.

Preheat the oven to 170°C (fan)/190°C/375°F/Gas mark 5. Line a flat baking tray with parchment paper.

Roll out the dough on a lightly floured work surface to a thickness of about 5mm/¼in with a 5cm/2in round pastry cutter. Take half of the circles and make a small hole with a tiny cutter or a small nozzle of a piping bag in the centre. On the circles without holes, place a dollop of jam. Sandwich with other circles (ones with the hole). The jam should be visible, but be careful not to press too hard as it will escape during cooking.

Place the biscuits on the prepared baking tray, sprinkle with caster sugar and bake in the oven for about 15 minutes until golden.

Remove from the oven and leave to cool. Store in an airtight container for up to a week.

Quick and simple to make, these biscuits are a joy to eat! The dough is delicate and just like the Basic Biscuits (see p.182) with the addition of orange zest. Once cooked, they are sandwiched together with Nutella spread, which I am sure the kids will love to help out to make! They will keep for a week if stored properly, but I doubt they will last that long!

BISCOTTI ALLA NUTELLA
Nutella Biscuits

Makes 11 biscuits

150g/5½oz/1¼ cups plain (all-purpose) flour
100g/3½oz/7 tbsp cold unsalted butter, cut into
    small chunks
70g/2½oz/⅔ cup icing (confectioners') sugar, sifted,
    plus extra for sprinkling
grated zest of ½ orange
seeds of ½ vanilla pod (bean)
1 egg yolk
about ½ small jar (about 100g/3½oz) of Nutella

Sift the flour into a bowl, add the butter and rub it in until it resembles breadcrumbs. Mix in the icing sugar, orange zest and vanilla seeds. Add the egg yolk and work into a smooth dough, working quickly to avoid the dough getting warm. Form the dough into a ball, wrap in clingfilm and leave to chill for at least 30 minutes, or until required.

Preheat the oven to 170°C (fan)/190°C/375°F/Gas mark 5. Line 2 flat baking trays with parchment paper.

Roll out the dough on a floured work surface to a thickness of about 5mm/¼in. Using a 5cm/2in round pastry cutter, cut out 22 circles and place on the prepared baking tray. Bake in the oven for about 10 minutes until golden.

Remove from the oven, leave to cool, then sandwich together with some Nutella. Arrange on a plate and sprinkle with a little icing sugar. Store in an airtight container for up to a week.

These biscuits come from Castellamare, the hometown of my mother. They were always a treat when we went to visit my grandparents or if they came to visit us. We would eat them dipped in our morning milk or at teatime with hot chocolate. I really wanted to recreate them for this book as they evoke happy childhood memories and they are not the sort of biscuit you can easily find except if you go to this particular town. They are made with a leavened dough and traditionally with the local carbonated spring water. For the purposes of recreating the recipe at home, I used Badoit mineral water, which is only slightly sparkling.

BISCOTTI DI CASTELLAMARE
Childhood Biscuits

Makes about 16 biscuits

FOR THE STARTER DOUGH:
12g/¼oz fresh yeast
40ml/1½fl oz/3 tbsp
    lukewarm water
150g/5½oz/1¼ cups strong
    white bread flour
FOR THE BISCUITS:
250g/9oz/2 cups strong
    white bread flour
90g/3¼oz/½ cup caster
    (superfine) sugar
40g/1½oz/3 tbsp unsalted
    butter, softened at room
    temperature
grated zest of ½ lemon
120ml/4fl oz/½ cup
    naturally carbonated
    water (e.g. Badoit)
FOR DUSTING:
about 2 tsp icing
    (confectioners') sugar,
    sifted
½ tsp ground cinnamon

First make the starter dough. Dissolve the yeast in the lukewarm water, add the flour and mix well to form a dough. Knead into a ball, cover with clingfilm, and leave to rest in a warm place for 1 hour.

Preheat the oven to 170°C (fan)/190°C/375°F/Gas mark 5. Line a flat baking tray with parchment paper.

Place the starter dough on a work surface, open it out a little and knead in the rest of the biscuit ingredients until everything is well incorporated and a smooth dough has formed.

Roll pieces of the dough into cigar-type shapes of about 15cm/6in long. Place on the prepared tray, cover with a cloth and leave to rest at room temperature for 10 minutes.

Mix the icing sugar and cinnamon together and sprinkle over the top of the biscuits. Bake for about 25–30 minutes until golden.

Remove from the oven and leave to cool. Can be stored in an airtight container for up to a week.

Also known as *bussolai* or *buranelli*, these simple but tasty biscuits originate from the lovely Venetian island of Burano where traditionally they were made during Easter. They are now very popular around Venice all year round and found wrapped in cellophane and sold in bakeries or offered at the end of a meal in restaurants with a glass of sweet dessert wine. They are made into an 'S' shape or can also be round rings.

BISCOTTI VENEZIANI BURANELLI
Venetian Biscuits

Makes about 22 biscuits

250g/9oz/2 cups plain (all-purpose) flour
pinch of salt
75g/2¾oz/⅓ cup unsalted butter,
    softened at room temperature
100g/3½oz/½ cup caster (superfine) sugar
3 egg yolks, beaten
1 tsp vanilla extract
1 tbsp rum
grated zest of 1 lemon

Sift the flour and salt into a large bowl. Add the remaining ingredients and mix well to form a smooth dough. Wrap in clingfilm and leave to chill for at least 30 minutes.

Meanwhile, preheat the oven to 160°C (fan)/180°C/350°F/Gas mark 4. Line 2 large flat baking trays with parchment paper.

Place the dough on a lightly floured work surface. Slice off a piece of dough and roll out in a long thin sausage shape and cut out 12cm/4½in lengths which you form into 'S' shapes. Continue doing this with the rest of the pastry. Place the biscuits on the prepared tray and bake in the oven for about 15–20 minutes until golden.

Remove from the oven and leave to cool slightly. Store in an airtight container for up to a week.

Very simple to make, but make sure you use the best lemons you can get for ideal results – if you find them, use Amalfi lemons – a good greengrocer will be able to get them for you. If you prefer, you can omit the icing and enjoy the biscuits plain, you will still taste the lemony tang from the zest in the dough.

BISCOTTI AL LIMONE
Lemon Biscuits

Makes about 22 biscuits

150g/5½oz/1¼ cups plain (all-purpose) flour
100g/3½oz/7 tbsp cold unsalted butter, cut into
    small chunks
70g/2½oz/⅔ cup icing (confectioners') sugar, sifted
grated zest of 2 lemons
1 egg yolk
FOR THE LEMON GLAZE:
75g/2¾oz/⅔ cup icing (confectioners') sugar
juice of ½ lemon
grated zest of 1 lemon

Sift the flour into a bowl, add the butter and rub it in until it resembles breadcrumbs. Mix in the icing sugar and lemon zest. Add the egg yolk and work into a smooth dough, working quickly to avoid the dough getting warm. Form the dough into a ball, wrap in clingfilm and chill for at least 30 minutes, or until required.

Preheat the oven to 170°C (fan)/190°C/375°F/Gas mark 5. Line a flat baking tray with parchment paper.

Roll out the dough on a lightly floured work surface to a thickness of about 5mm/¼in. Using a 5cm/2in round pastry cutter (or any shaped cutter you prefer), cut the dough into circles and place onto the prepared baking tray. Bake in the oven for about 10 minutes until lightly golden.

Remove from the oven and leave to cool for 2 minutes on the baking tray, then transfer to a wire rack to cool completely.

To make the glaze, sift the icing sugar into a bowl and gradually add enough lemon juice to make a smooth icing (you may need more or less juice). Stir in the zest, then drizzle the icing over the biscuits. Leave to set for 20–30 minutes. Can be stored in an airtight container for up to a week.

These typical Italian cookies date back to the early 1800s when they were made during Easter in the shape of little baskets and children would put coloured eggs inside. Over time, these popular biscuits have evolved into a flower shape and are eaten at any time. They are made industrially sold in packets in shops and supermarkets all over Italy and exported abroad. However, the homemade version is so much tastier. The combination of potato flour and the unusual addition of hard-boiled egg yolks give these biscuits their lovely characteristic crumbly melt-in-your-mouth texture. Once you start eating, you will not be able to stop!

CANESTRELLI
Flower-Shaped Biscuits

Makes about 50 biscuits

4 egg yolks
200g/7oz/1⅔ cups plain (all-purpose) flour, sifted
150g/5½oz/1¼ cups potato flour
200g/7oz/scant 1 cup cold unsalted butter,
   cut into pieces
100g/3½oz/scant 1 cup icing (confectioners') sugar,
   plus extra for dusting
2 tsp vanilla extract
grated zest of 1 lemon

Cook the eggs until hard-boiled, leave to cool, then remove the shell and discard the whites. Crumble up the yolks and set aside.

Combine the flours in a large bowl, add the butter, and rub it in until it resembles breadcrumbs. Stir in the icing sugar, vanilla and lemon zest, then sieve in the egg yolks. Mix well to form a very smooth dough, then wrap in clingfilm and leave to chill for 1 hour.

Preheat the oven to 150°C (fan)/170°C/325°F/Gas mark 3. Line a flat baking tray with parchment paper.

Roll out the dough on a floured work surface to a thickness of 1cm/½in. Cut out flower shapes using a 5cm/2in round flower cutter, then cut out a small circle with the bottom end of small nozzle of a piping bag in the centre. Place on the prepared baking tray and bake for 17–20 minutes until just becoming golden.

Remove from the oven, leave to cool, then sprinkle with icing sugar. Store in an airtight container for 2 weeks.

These Tuscan speciality biscuits originate from the city of Siena and are traditionally given as gifts at Christmas. However, there is no reason why you can't enjoy these slightly chewy almond-based treats at any time. They date back from ancient times when a noble knight, Ricciardetto della Gheradesca, returned home from the Crusades. To celebrate his safe return, these biscuits were created, using almonds from the Middle East and with their pointed shape resembling Turkish slippers. The original recipe is made with ground bitter almonds; however, normal ground almonds with a few drops of almond extract are equally delicious. As no flour is used, they are ideal for anyone on a gluten-free diet. Nowadays, they are commercially made and widely available in good pastry shops all over Italy, however, they are so simple to make and you can add less sugar to suit your taste.

RICCIARELLI
Tuscan Almond Biscuits (Gluten-free)

Makes about 15 biscuits

250g/9oz/2¾ cups ground almonds
180g/6oz/1½ cups icing (confectioners') sugar,
   plus extra for dusting
1 tsp almond or vanilla extract
whites of 2 small eggs

Combine the ground almonds and icing sugar in a large bowl, then add the vanilla extract.

In another bowl, whisk the egg whites until stiff. Fold the egg whites into the ground almond mixture until a sticky dough has formed. Don't worry if it feels a little too sticky. Wrap the dough in clingfilm and leave to chill overnight or for at least 12 hours.

Preheat the oven to 150°C (fan)/170°C/325°F/Gas mark 3. Line a large flat baking tray with parchment paper.

Lightly dust a work surface with some icing sugar and, using your hands, roll the dough into a long thick sausage shape. Cut out chunks weighing about 30g/1oz each, then flatten and form into diamond shapes, roughly 1cm/½in thick and 10cm/4in in length. Dust each all over with abundant icing sugar, then place on the prepared baking tray.

Bake the biscuits in the oven for 12 minutes. Do not allow them to colour; these biscuits are supposed to be white. Remove from the oven, leave to cool for a few minutes on the baking tray, then transfer to a wire rack to cool completely. Enjoy or store in an airtight container for up to a week.

The classic Tuscan *Cantucci* biscuits have evolved quite a lot over the last few years. Originally with almonds and used to dip into the sweet wine Vin Santo for special occasions, now you can add all sorts of different ingredients and flavours. I especially like these with pistachio nuts and pieces of white chocolate, which I enjoy with a mid-morning cappuccino.

CANTUCCINI CON PISTACCHIO E CIOCCOLATO BIANCO
Cantuccini with Pistachio and White Chocolate

Makes about 24

150g/5½oz/1 cup pistachio nuts
300g/10½oz/2½ cups plain (all-purpose) flour, sifted
½ tsp baking powder, sifted
pinch of salt
2 eggs
80g/3oz/scant ½ cup caster (superfine) sugar
60ml/2fl oz/¼ cup double (heavy) cream
100g/3½oz white chocolate, roughly chopped

Preheat the oven to 200°C (fan)/220°C/425°F/Gas mark 7.

Place the pistachio nuts on a baking tray and roast in the oven for 10 minutes. Remove and set aside.

Turn the oven down to 170°C (fan)/190°C/375°F/Gas mark 5. Line a large flat baking tray with parchment paper.

Sift the flour, baking powder and salt together.

Whisk the eggs and sugar together in a large bowl until light and creamy. Stir in the cream, then fold in the flour mixture. Add the chocolate and roasted pistachios and mix well to form a dough.

Divide the dough in half and roll each one into a long sausage about 35cm/14in long and 5cm/2in wide. Place on the prepared baking tray and bake in the oven for 15 minutes.

Remove from the oven and cut each sausage diagonally into slices of about 2cm/¾in with a sharp knife. Lay them flat on the baking tray and return to the oven for a further 10 minutes, or until crunchy. Remove from the oven, leave to cool and serve or store in an airtight container for up to a week.

These traditional Neapolitan biscuits have been around for centuries and are normally prepared at Christmas time. The name comes from 'mosto' as this was traditionally used to sweeten them. They are made in the classical diamond shape and sold in confectionery shops all over the region. For me, they symbolise Christmas and I always make sure I have some to remind me of home. I have given you a large quantity because it was always traditional in Italy to make lots and give them away to family and friends as gifts. You don't have to make the full quantity but if you do, you can always freeze the dough. To give them more of a Christmas twist, I have made them into star shapes.

MOSTACCIOLI
Christmas Biscuits

Makes about 60 biscuits

1kg/2lb 4oz/8⅓ cups plain (all-purpose) flour, sifted
2 tsp baking powder, sifted
600g/1lb 5oz/3 cups caster (superfine) sugar
15g/½oz mixed spice
300g/10½oz/3⅓ cups ground almonds
50g/1¾oz/½ cup cocoa powder, sifted
200ml/7fl oz/½ cup runny honey
200g/7oz/generous ½ cup apricot jam
175ml/6oz/¾ cup sweet wine (e.g. Marsala, or Vin Santo)
175ml/6oz/¾ cup water
FOR THE TOPPING:
about 1.2kg/2lb 12oz dark chocolate (at least 70% cocoa solids), broken into pieces

Combine all the ingredients together in a large bowl or on a clean work surface and mix into a smooth dough. Form into a ball, wrap in clingfilm and leave to chill for 24 hours.

Preheat the oven to 160°C (fan)/180°C/350°F/Gas mark 4. Line a large flat baking tray with parchment paper.

Roll out the dough paper on a lightly floured work surface to a thickness of 1cm/½in and cut out star shapes with a 10cm/4in star-shaped cutter. Brush off any excess flour with a little water. Place on the prepared baking trays and bake in the oven for 20 minutes.

Remove from the oven and leave to cool for a few minutes on the tray, then transfer to a wire rack to cool completely.

For the topping, melt the chocolate in a heatproof bowl set over a pan of gently simmering water. Make sure the base of the bowl doesn't touch the water. Dip the biscuits into the melted chocolate to cover completely and leave to set overnight on parchment paper. Store in an airtight container for up to a month.

Almond-based cakes and biscuits are typical of Sicily where almonds grow in abundance. Traditionally these biscuits are made for special occasions such as weddings and christenings where they are made in different colours. Simple and quick to make, they do look very pretty, and you can colour and decorate as you like. If you prefer to keep them plain, they are just as delicious. They are also perfect for anyone with a gluten intolerance!

PASTICCINI DI MANDORLA SICILIANI COLORATI
Sicilian Coloured Almond Biscuits

Makes about 24

2 egg whites
250g/9oz/2¾ cups ground
    almonds
220g/7¾oz/generous
    1 cup caster (superfine)
    sugar
2 tsp runny honey
4 drops of almond extract
grated zest of 1 orange
green and red food
    colouring
a little sifted icing
    (confectioners') sugar and
    caster (superfine) sugar
    for sprinkling
glacé (candied) cherries,
    angelica and whole
    almonds, to decorate

Preheat the oven to 160°C (fan)/180°C/350°F/Gas mark 4. Line a large baking tray with parchment paper.

Whisk the egg whites until nearly stiff, then set aside.

Combine the ground almonds and sugar in a large bowl, then add the honey, almond extract and orange zest. Fold in the egg whites and mix gently until a smooth, sticky dough-like consistency has formed.

Divide the mixture into 3 portions. Add a few drops of red colouring to one piece and knead it in until it is a uniform colour. Do the same with the green food colouring, and leave one piece in its natural colour.

Place one coloured mixture into a piping bag fitted with a large star-shaped nozzle and pipe out rosettes, about 5cm/2in in diameter, onto the prepared baking tray. Do the same with the next colour and the one after. Please note the mixture is quite stiff so a little patience is needed while piping, but the effort will be worth it!

Mix the icing and caster sugars together and sprinkle over the rosettes, then decorate with pieces of cherry, angelica and almonds. Bake in the oven for 7–10 minutes until just beginning to colour.

Remove from the oven and leave to cool, during which time the biscuits will harden slightly. Store in an airtight container for up to a week.

These classic light sponge fingers are widely used in preparing Italian desserts such as *tiramisu* and *zuppa inglese*. However, they are also lovely eaten on their own with tea or dipped in a cappuccino. Being fat-free and easily digestible, *Savoiardi* are a popular choice in Italy with young children, convalescents and the elderly. Although industrially produced and found in most shops, they are very simple and quick to make at home and of course taste much nicer.

SAVOIARDI ALLA VANIGLIA
Vanilla Sponge Fingers

Makes about 20 biscuits

70g/2½oz/generous ⅓ cup caster (superfine) sugar
2 eggs, separated
35g/1¼oz/generous ¼ cup plain (all-purpose) flour, sifted
2 tsp potato flour, sifted
pinch of salt
seeds of 1 vanilla pod (bean)
2 tsp icing (confectioners') sugar, sifted

Preheat the oven to 180°C (fan)/200°C/400°F/Gas mark 6. Line 2 large flat baking trays with parchment paper.

Place 30g/1oz/2 tablespoons of the sugar and the egg yolks in a bowl and whisk until light and creamy. In another clean bowl, whisk 30g/1oz/2 tablespoons of the sugar and the egg whites until stiffened.

Combine the flours and salt together and then fold into the egg yolk mixture. Add the vanilla seeds, then fold in the stiffened egg whites until everything is well incorporated.

Place the mixture into a piping bag fitted with a smooth nozzle and pipe 10cm/4in fingers on the prepared baking tray, spacing them apart as they expand while baking.

Mix the remaining caster sugar and the icing sugar together and sprinkle all over the *savoiardi*. Bake for 10 minutes until golden. Store in an airtight container for up to a week.

TORTE
Cakes

Who can possibly resist a homemade cake?

Traditionally cakes were not as we know them today – often the only factor that put them in the cake category was a round shape. They tended to be more bread-like with perhaps the addition of honey to sweeten it. The ancient Romans added butter and eggs, and a more cake-like consistency and texture were evident, but still nothing like the cakes we know and love today.

As with all food, cakes, too, have evolved throughout the ages but the basic ingredients of flour, sugar, eggs and butter are the norm in most cakes. Some cakes in Italy omit butter and the eggs are often separated, with the yolks being whisked with sugar and the whites whisked until stiff, flour is then folded in and the three ingredients combined. This whisking method results in a light fat-free sponge known as *pan di spagna* and forms the basis of so many celebration cakes, which are filled and decorated according to the occasion. These are popular in cake shops throughout Italy as well as easy to make at home.

Olive oil is a popular addition to Italian cakes and has long been used by housewives, resulting in a deliciously moist cake. Ricotta and plain yogurt are also popular healthy additions.

As in most parts of the world, a cake usually symbolises a celebration, from simple homemade sponges for a child's birthday to fancy wedding cakes. Over the years, cakes have become more elaborate and even a child's birthday cake is themed with superhero or cartoon characters or a sport. When I was a child, a plain homemade sponge dusted with icing sugar was the norm. Nowadays with an abundance of food colourings, sugar paste and unusually shaped tins all readily available in cook shops and online, we can get creative and make cakes to impress.

Cakes with fresh fruit added to them are popular in Italy and a homely apple or pear cake makes a nice teatime treat. When you hear Italians talking about plum cake (see p.213), this has nothing to do with the addition of plums. They mean a cake which is baked in a loaf tin and usually has a little dried fruit or chocolate chips added to it.

Despite all the advances in cake making, I still prefer a simple cake like a plain sponge or olive oil cake, and it doesn't have to be a birthday or anniversary to enjoy it. Homemade cakes are a pleasure at any time, and because they are so simple, good-quality ingredients are important in achieving the best results. Try to get good-quality flour, if possible, and caster sugar, good-quality butter and organic free-range eggs. I remember as a child, the colour of cake sponge was always a lovely yellow because the eggs were so fresh and good. Whenever I'm in the countryside, I always stock up on the freshest of farm eggs, and there is nothing more delicious than a simple cake made with good ingredients.

TIPS FOR CAKE MAKING

• Use the best ingredients you can afford, especially butter and eggs; they will really enhance the taste of your cake.

• Preheat the oven at the correct temperature.

• Use the correct size tin as specified in the recipe.

• Remember to line and grease your tins accordingly.

• If the recipe asks for separating the eggs – make sure you whisk the yolks and sugar really well and for a good 5 minutes, even with an electric whisk, until light, creamy, and you can almost make patterns with the mixture. Wash your whisk blades and whisk the whites until stiff in a clean, dry bowl.

• Make sure you have a long enough wooden skewer to hand for inserting into the cake to check if it is cooked.

• Always leave the cake to cool completely before decorating or dusting with icing sugar.

Despite its name, this is a typical Italian sponge, which is made for birthday and celebration cakes as well as the base for many desserts. After baking and left to cool until cold, the sponge is drizzled with a syrup of water and alcohol to moisten it; if making for kids, you can substitute the alcohol with freshly squeezed orange, although the alcohol content is so diluted it really will not harm. I tend to use Marsala, as it's easier to find, but you can use Strega or Maraschino. The typical filling is a vanilla-flavoured custard cream (*crème patissiere*) and cocoa powder can be added for a chocolatey flavour. For a special cake, three or four layers of sponge are made with alternating custard-flavoured fillings and the top decorated with mixed fruit. If you prefer, you can sandwich the layers with whipped cream and/or jam. I often like to make a plain sponge without the syrup and filling, and enjoy a slice or two with my morning espresso for breakfast. If you want to do the same, just use half this quantity and bake in a 20cm/8in sponge tin for about 20–25 minutes. For a delicious sponge, please use the best quality free-range organic eggs you can get. It is the traditional lengthy whisking of the eggs and sugar which gives air to the cake, making it rise and therefore not needing any additional rising agents.

TORTA PAN DI SPAGNA
Italian Sponge Cake

Serves 8

FOR THE SPONGE:
180g/6oz/scant 1 cup caster (superfine) sugar
6 eggs
pinch of salt
1 tsp vanilla extract
180g/6oz/scant 1½ cups plain (all-purpose) flour, sifted
FOR THE FILLING:
250ml/9fl oz/generous 1 cup milk
½ vanilla pod (bean)
3 egg yolks
100g/3½oz/½ cup caster (superfine) sugar
25g/1oz/scant ¼ cup cornflour (cornstarch)
FOR THE SYRUP:
300ml/10fl oz/1¼ cups water
70ml/2½fl oz/scant ⅓ cup Marsala
2 tbsp caster (superfine) sugar
3 slices orange rind
3 slices lemon rind

<<

Preheat the oven to 160°C (fan)/180°C/350°F/Gas mark 4. Lightly grease a 26cm/10½in round cake tin, then dust with flour.

Using an electric whisk, beat the sugar and eggs together until light and creamy for about 15 minutes and the mixture reaches the 'ribbon' stage (when the whisk is lifted over the bowl, the mixture falls back slowly forming a ribbon that will hold its shape for a few minutes). About halfway through whisking, add the salt and vanilla. Using a spatula, fold in the flour gradually and gently until it is incorporated. Pour the mixture into the prepared tin and bake in the oven for 40 minutes until golden. Insert a wooden skewer to check if cooked through; if it comes out clean, the cake is cooked.

Remove from the oven, leave to cool for a few minutes, then turn out of the tin and leave to cool completely on a wire rack. Once cold, carefully slice in half. Set aside.

To make the filling, pour the milk into a small saucepan, add the vanilla pod and heat until the milk reaches boiling point. Meanwhile, whisk the egg yolks and sugar together in a large bowl until light and fluffy. Add the cornflour and continue to whisk, then gradually pour the hot milk into the egg mixture, whisking constantly to prevent lumps forming. Once combined, pour the mixture back into the saucepan, place over a medium heat and stir with a wooden spoon. As soon as it begins to boil, remove from the heat, pour into a dish and leave to cool.

To make the syrup, put all the ingredients into a small pan over a medium heat, stirring all the time until the sugar has dissolved and the liquid has reduced by about one-third. Remove from the heat and leave to cool completely. Discard the rinds. Drizzle or brush the syrup over both layers of sponge.

Place one layer on a plate and spread with the custard filling, then sandwich together with the other layer of sponge. Decorate as you wish.

Fresh fruit is often added to cakes in Italy, and I remember my grandma making a similar cake to this one using apples. It's a great way of adding more fruit to your diet, especially for children. Pear and dark chocolate go really well together and this makes a lovely cake to serve for afternoon tea.

TORTA DI PERE E CIOCCOLATO
Pear and Chocolate Cake

Serves 6–8

3 eggs
150g/5½oz/¾ cup caster (superfine) sugar
85g/3oz/6 tbsp unsalted butter, room temperature
300g/10½oz/scant 2½ cups self-raising flour, sifted
seeds of 1 vanilla pod (bean)
grated zest of 1 small unwaxed lemon
3 ripe pears, peeled, cored and cut into chunks
75g/2¾oz dark chocolate (at least 70% cocoa
    solids), roughly broken into small chunks
FOR DECORATION:
100g/3½oz/½ cup caster (superfine) sugar
1 tbsp unsalted butter
2 pears, sliced very thinly,
a little sifted icing (confectioners') sugar (optional)

Preheat oven to 180°C (fan)/200°C/400°F/Gas mark 6. Grease a 20cm/ 8in round loose-bottomed cake tin, and line with parchment paper.

Whisk the eggs and sugar together in a large bowl until light and fluffy. Add the softened butter and continue to whisk until it is well amalgamated. Fold in the flour, vanilla, lemon zest, pears and chocolate. Pour the mixture into the prepared tin and bake in the oven for about 45 minutes. Insert a wooden skewer to check if cooked through, if it comes out clean, the cake is cooked. Remove from the oven and leave to cool. Loosen the cake and place on a serving plate.

To decorate, heat the sugar in a wide sauté pan over a medium heat. Do not stir, just gently agitate the pan from time to time until the sugar starts to melt; this will take about 5 minutes. Continue to cook, gently stirring with a wooden spoon for about 10 minutes, until a dark caramel forms. Stir the butter through and add the thinly sliced pears, turning to coat in the caramel. Cook for 3–4 minutes, until golden. Arrange on top of the cake. Decorate with sifted icing sugar, if liked.

This delicious gluten-free cake originates from the town of Varese in the northern Lombardy region of Italy where traditionally polenta was their main staple. Also known as *Dolce di Varese*, it was a popular Sunday treat and is now sold in pastry shops and cafés all over the region. Quick and easy to prepare, this almond-infused cake makes a lovely teatime treat. .

AMOR DI POLENTA!
Polenta and Almond Cake (Gluten-free)

Serves 6

100g/3½oz/7 tbsp unsalted butter, softened at
    room temperature
100g/3½oz/½ cup caster (superfine) sugar
2 eggs, lightly beaten
100g/3½oz/scant 1 cup instant polenta (cornmeal)
80g/3oz/⅔ cup gluten-free plain (all-purpose)
    white flour (such as Doves)
1 tsp gluten-free baking powder (such as Doves)
75g/2¾oz/scant 1 cup ground almonds
1 tsp vanilla extract
1 tbsp Amaretto liqueur

Preheat the oven to 160°C (fan)/180°C/350°F/Gas mark 4 and line a 19 x 8cm/7½ x 3¼in loaf tin with parchment paper.

Whisk the butter and sugar together in a large bowl until creamy. Gradually add the eggs, then fold in the flours, baking powder and ground almonds. Add the vanilla and Amaretto, and fold in until it is incorporated.

Pour the mixture into the prepared loaf tin and bake in the oven for 35 minutes until golden brown. Insert a wooden skewer to check if cooked through; if it comes out clean, the cake is cooked.

Remove from the oven, leave to cool slightly before turning out from the tin.

This is a twist on the traditional olive oil cake, which Italian housewives would often make. Years ago, olive oil was used instead of butter to make a plain and simple homemade cake. The addition of olive oil to a cake gives it a much lighter texture with all the added health benefits. I have taken the basic recipe and added some lemon and rosemary, and serving a raspberry coulis alongside the cake makes this a lovely dessert. You can of course replace the lemon and rosemary with grated orange zest or grated chocolate or any other flavour you prefer. The coulis can be made with strawberries or a selection of mixed berries.

TORTA ALL'OLIO CON LIMONE E ROSMARINO SERVITA CON SALSINA DI LAMPONI

Olive Oil Cake with Lemon and Rosemary Served with a Raspberry Coulis

Serves 6

175g/6oz/scant 1½ cups self-raising flour, sifted
175g/6oz/scant 1 cup caster (superfine) sugar
grated zest of 2 large lemons
2 tsp finely chopped rosemary needles
220ml/7½fl oz/scant 1 cup olive oil
5 eggs, lightly beaten
a little icing (confectioners') sugar, sifted
FOR THE RASPBERRY COULIS (OPTIONAL):
200g/7oz/1⅔ cups raspberries
50g/1¾oz/scant ¼ cup caster (superfine) sugar
juice of 1 red-blood orange

Preheat the oven to 140°C (fan)/160°C/325°F/Gas mark 3 and line a 20cm/8in round loose-bottomed cake tin with parchment paper.

Mix the flour, sugar, lemon zest and rosemary together in a large bowl. Add the olive oil and eggs, and whisk until it is all well incorporated. Pour the mixture into the prepared cake tin and bake on the bottom part of the oven for 55–60 minutes. Insert a wooden skewer to check if cooked through; if it comes out clean, the cake is cooked.

Remove from the oven, cool slightly, then tip the cake out of the tin and leave to cool completely on a wire rack before dusting with icing sugar.

To make the coulis, place all the ingredients in a small pan, setting aside a few of the raspberries. Simmer over a medium heat for about 7 minutes, or until the sauce begins to thicken. Remove from the heat, leave to cool slightly, stir in the whole raspberries and serve with the cake, if liked.

In Italy, plum cake does not mean the inclusion of plums in a cake! It refers to a cake such as this one cooked in a loaf tin usually made with dried fruit. However, on a recent visit to my hometown, my niece made this lovely chocolate chip cake and referred to it as plum cake. A similar cake was served at breakfast at the hotel I was staying at, and Liz and my daughters couldn't get enough of it! So I decided it was only right to include this cake in this book and dedicate it to Anna, my niece. Made with ricotta and no butter, it is healthy and light and delicious at teatime or for breakfast.

PLUM CAKE DI ANNA
Chocolate Chip and Ricotta Loaf Cake

Serves 6–8

250g/9oz/generous 1 cup ricotta
250g/9oz/1¼ cups caster (superfine) sugar
4 eggs, separated
seeds of 1 vanilla pod (bean)
250g/9oz/2 cups self-raising flour, sifted
pinch of salt
80g/3oz dark chocolate chips

Preheat the oven to 160°C (fan)/180°C/350°F/Gas mark 4, and line a 24 x 13cm/9½ x 5in loaf tin with parchment paper.

Whisk the ricotta and sugar together in a large bowl, then add the egg yolks and continue to whisk until light and creamy. Stir in vanilla seeds, then fold in flour and salt. Add the chocolate drops.

In a separate bowl, whisk the egg whites until stiff, then fold the egg whites into the cake mixture until it is well incorporated. Pour the mixture into the prepared tin and bake in the oven for about 50–60 minutes. Insert a wooden skewer to check if cooked through; if it comes out clean, the cake is cooked. If you notice the cake browning too much on the top, but it is still not ready, cover the top with foil and continue baking.

Remove from the oven, leave to cool, then tip the cake out of the tin and serve.

This typical *ciambella* has all the taste of a rustic, homemade Italian cake made in the traditional ring tin. Made with olive oil instead of butter, the addition of yogurt makes it a very light and delicate sponge. Be careful when removing it from the tin – it is so soft and light, it can easily break. Whenever I make this, it reminds me of the cakes my aunts and older sisters would make when I was a little boy. So simple, it is a perfect cake for afternoon tea.

CIAMBELLA ALLO YOGURT E ARANCIA
Yogurt and Orange Ring Cake

Serves 10

300g/10½oz/1½ cups caster (superfine) sugar
3 large eggs
juice of 1 orange
grated zest of 1 orange
250ml/9fl oz/generous 1 cup olive oil
100g/3½oz/scant ½ cup good-quality plain yogurt
300g/10½oz/scant 2½ cups self-raising flour, sifted
1 tsp baking powder, sifted
FOR THE TOPPING:
6 tbsp plain yogurt
seeds of 1 vanilla pod (bean)
grated zest and juice of 1 orange
1 tbsp sifted icing (confectioners') sugar
orange peel, to decorate

Preheat the oven to 180°C (fan)/200°C/400°F/Gas mark 6. Grease a 26cm/10½in round ring tin and dust with flour.

Whisk the sugar and eggs together in a large bowl until creamy and the mixture turns a pale colour. Add the orange juice and zest, olive oil and yogurt and continue to whisk. Fold in the flour and baking powder until it is all well incorporated. Pour the mixture into the prepared tin and bake for 40–45 minutes until well risen and golden. Insert a wooden skewer to check if cooked through; if it comes out clean, the cake is cooked.

Remove from the oven, leave to cool completely, then turn the cake out of the tin.

To make the topping, combine the yogurt, vanilla, orange juice and zest and icing sugar. Pour over the cake and decorate with orange peel.

I love marble cake with a mix of plain sponge and chocolate. To give it a bit of an Italian twist, I have added some espresso coffee and instead of the usual ring tin, I have made it into a loaf shape. Light and delicate, it makes a perfect accompaniment to your mid-morning cup of espresso.

DOLCE MARMORIZZATO ALL'ESPRESSO
Marbled Espresso Loaf Cake

Serves 6

1 strong espresso coffee (about 60ml/2fl oz/½ cup)
4 tbsp lukewarm milk
seeds of ½ vanilla pod (bean) or 1 tsp vanilla extract
4 eggs, separated
210g/7oz/scant 1 cup unsalted butter, softened at
    room temperature
230g/8oz/generous 1 cup caster (superfine) sugar
240g/8oz/scant 2 cups self-raising flour, sifted
30g/1oz/⅓ cup cocoa powder, sifted
icing (confectioners') sugar

Preheat the oven to 160°C (fan)/180°C/350°F/Gas mark 4. Grease a 20 x 10cm/8 x 4in loaf tin and line with parchment paper.

Combine the espresso coffee with 2 tablespoons of milk and the vanilla in a small bowl. Set aside.

Whisk the butter and half of the sugar together in a large bowl until light and fluffy. In a separate bowl, whisk the egg yolks and remaining sugar until creamy. Combine both mixtures together, then fold in the flour. Pour half of the mixture into another bowl. In one bowl, add the espresso mixture. In the other bowl, stir in the cocoa powder and remaining milk. In a separate clean bowl, whisk the egg whites until stiff, then divide between the mixtures, folding in well.

Place alternate dollops of the mixtures in the prepared tin and level the surface. Bake for 1 hour, or until well risen. Insert a wooden skewer to check if cooked through; if it comes out clean, the cake is done.

Remove from the oven, leave to cool, then turn onto a plate. Sift icing sugar over the top and serve in slices.

This traditional gluten-free chestnut speciality is very common during autumn in the regions of Emilia Romagna, Liguria and Tuscany where chestnuts are abundant and said to be the best in Italy. It has age-old roots as chestnuts were once food of the poor – chestnuts were ground into flour and made into all sorts of dishes including a cake-type dish such as this one with the addition of water and rosemary, and as a treat some dried fruit would be added. Over time, as with all poor-man's dishes, this has become a sought-after delicacy enriched with milk, pine kernels, and I like to add a little dark chocolate. Unless you want to grind your own chestnuts, the flour is available from good delis.

CASTAGNACCIO
Chestnut Squares

Makes 8 squares

15g/½oz/2 tbsp raisins
Marsala or sweet wine, for soaking
200g/7oz/scant 1⅔ cups chestnut flour
pinch of salt
40g/1½oz/scant ¼ cup caster (superfine) sugar
450ml/16fl oz/2 cups milk
2 tbsp extra virgin olive oil
20g/¾oz/scant ¼ cup pine kernels
needles of 1 rosemary sprig
40g/1½oz dark chocolate shavings (at least 70% cocoa solids)

Preheat the oven to 180°C (fan)/200°C/400°F/Gas mark 6 and grease a 20 x 30cm/8 x 12in shallow roasting tine with extra virgin olive oil.

Soak the raisins for the filling in enough Marsala or other sweet wine to just cover.

Combine the flour, salt and sugar in a large bowl. Gradually whisk in the milk, extra virgin olive oil and 1 tablespoon of the Marsala, whisking well to avoid lumps. Stir in the pine kernels, raisins, rosemary needles and half of the chocolate. Pour the mixture into the prepared tin, top with the remaining chocolate shavings and bake in the oven for 30 minutes. Insert a wooden skewer to check if cooked through; if it comes out clean, the cake is cooked.

Remove from the oven, leave to cool in the tin, then cut into squares.

INDEX

ACKNOWLEDGEMENTS

Thanks to Liz Przybylski for researching and writing, to Adriana Contaldo for testing recipes and recreating them during the shoots, to Dan Jones for the gorgeous photos, to Emily Ezekiel for exquisite food styling, to Alexander Breeze for the prop styling, to commissioning editor Emily Preece-Morrison for being lovely and efficient, to Laura Russell and Miranda Harvey for the fantastic design, and finally to Kathy Steer for correcting very efficiently and quickly!

First published in the United Kingdom in 2016 by Pavilion
1 Gower Street, London WC1E 6HD

Text © Gennaro Contaldo, 2016
Design and layout © Pavilion Books Company Ltd, 2016
Photography © Pavilion Books Company Ltd, 2016, except for images credited below

Location Image Credits
p.9 top left: © Anette Mossbacher/Alamy
p.9 top right: © John Heseltine/Alamy
p.9 bottom left: © John Heseltine/Alamy
p.9 bottom right and p.49: © Hemis/Alamy
p.204: © Ian Dagnall/Alamy

ISBN: 978-1-91090-435-0

A CIP catalogue record for this book is available from the British Library.

10 9 8 7 6 5 4 3 2 1

Reproduction by Mission Productions Ltd., Hong Kong
Printed and bound by 1010 Printing Group Ltd., China

This book can be ordered direct from the publisher at: www.pavilionbooks.com